Content

CW00644481

Foreword
Paul Claudel

I've known Pierre Casse for quite a few years, I have seen him teach, I have listened to him talk, I have read many of his lines. The words that immediately come to my mind, if I want to qualify this exceptional personality are: provocative, innovative, surprising, challenging, and often funny.

But let us not be misled: behind this unusual style of communication lies a keen observer and a deep thinker who has been exploring the ways and means of leadership and what it is that makes leaders succeed or fail.

It seems that for Pierre Casse, in this ever changing world, the biggest danger for a leader is to get stuck in the status quo: if you stay trapped in what has worked before, if you keep thinking in the same box (but it's not a question either of thinking out of the box, it's about getting rid of boxes altogether!), if you don't discover before the others what awaits you behind the corner, you are dead (to use one of his preferred expressions). So Casse's message is: constantly question your (and others') thinking, never take anything for granted, challenge your assumptions, look at it from a different angle. Sometimes you might find this constantly destabilising approach somewhat irritating, until having to accept that, well, after all, he may be right, he probably has a point, let's pay some attention here. And you end up with a new, different perspective, a mind opening idea and, whether you like it or not, a take on leadership that you can no longer ignore and which will probably force you to give a new twist to your practice of leading others.

In this book, Pierre Casse takes a fresh look at the leadership challenges facing in turn the business, then the corporation, before drawing a series of inevitable conclusions on how leaders need to develop new skills to face this newly emerging working environment.

The new aspects affecting the business context pertain to the facts that this global environment is changing in so many ways and so quickly that no leader is really capable of grasping all these factors and making sense of them in time enough to structure a rational, stable, durable action plan to lead the business. So what will be in need now and more and more is to grasp opportunities and move fast, to make use of intuition and courage, to be creative and reactive, to turn inevitable mistakes into opportunities. Regarding the corporate environment, new values and behaviours are also required: there is too much boredom at work, due to the leaders' lack of imagination in setting and communicating directions and challenges; the power game, inherent to all organisations, is too often brutal and crudely self-serving rather than prone to open exciting opportunities, and ethics are badly overridden; too many lies, too much corruption, too much abuse of fear.

To deal more effectively with these new business and corporate challenges, what will be required of leaders is a combination of traits revolving around courage, intuition, creativity, empathy and ethical behaviour, all building an exciting and productive working environment. Yes, all these traits have always been necessary, no doubt, but the way the Pierre Casse presents them makes them appear with a new sense of urgency, especially in contrast with what we can witness in most organizations today.

Going back to one of the terms I used above to qualify Pierre Casse's way of addressing leadership issues as being provocative, I believe that it would do him more justice to describe his approach as thought provoking. Going through this exciting book the reader will discover that rather than remembering Casse's lessons and ideas per se, he or she will progressively produce his/her own ideas for enhanced leadership as a result of the thinking process induced by this original and creative author.

Preface
Mark Stoddard

Business Leadership Review was first published online in April 2004. When I was first asked to launch a publication for the Association of MBAs a year earlier, my primary goal was to ensure that it was something that had intellectual gravitas while at the same time being provocative and stimulating; more engaging than a throw-away magazine while at the same time being more accessible and inclusive than a traditional journal.

I always knew that I would need help if there was any chance that the lofty aim of this project was to be realised, and Pierre Casse was always at the top of my list - we had done some work together and Pierre had published a paper in one of the early issues of BLR, and I won't deny that his reputation an internationally-renowned Professor of Leadership would be a major asset. When the time felt right to establish a formal Editorial Board for BLR to oversee its development and provide quality oversight, Pierre was the first person I approached. Since that time, Pierre's contribution to BLR has exceeded even my high expectations – his flurry of ideas to introduce innovative ways to bring the debate of leadership more firmly into the public domain has been inspiring and a driving force in ensuring that the Association of MBAs is at the forefront of these fundamentally important discussions.

'Casse's Corner' is one realisation of these ideas. Originally published as a regular column in BLR over the last few years, Pierre has written on a range of leadership topics, but always with the central goals of provocation, debate, reflection, accessibility, and action. He has never shied away from discussing the shortcomings of today's leaders, or of discussing controversial topics such as corruption, democracy and sexuality, but always with a focus on personal development and with a belief that the right leadership can bring substantial benefits to everyone, not just to business but also to the world at large.

Reflecting back at the ten year anniversary of *Business Leadership Review*, I know that there have been some missed opportunities but there is no doubt in my mind that the publication has made a valuable contribution to the debate on leadership in a range of contexts, and 'Casse's Corner' has been a key component in ensuring that we do not hide from discussing the real, complex and contentious issues facing leaders in today's ever-changing business and society contexts.

This collection of Pierre's 'Casse's Corner' columns is designed to provide you with an opportunity to pause for reflection, generate some new ideas, and most importantly provides a platform for transforming these ideas into practice. One of Pierre's central arguments is that the world needs more effective, ethical, transparent and transformative leaders – in business, politics, and society – and both Pierre and I hope that this book will contribute in some small part towards that goal.

Introduction
Pierre Casse

"Each concession we make is accompanied by an inner diminution of which we are not immediately conscious"

- Emile M Cioran

The aim of this book is to provide those leaders who are not afraid of questioning the way in which they think and behave with provocative ideas on subjects which can often prove sensitive. As such, the articles herein are aimed at leaders who enjoy a good challenge and who are always looking for opportunities to improve what they do and the way in which they do it.

In exploring the subject matter, the objective is not to be 'politically correct' but to 'throw caution to the wind' and adopt a rather direct tone. The articles are intended to stimulate thinking rather than convince readers of any particular position. In a sense the book constitutes a call to leaders in the field to question their usual way of thinking and behaving.

All too often, in the 'cut and thrust' of day-to-day business, leaders take situations for granted. They get used to approaching situations in a certain way because they feel comfortable rather than looking for opportunities to stimulate creativity. These articles are short and punchy and it is up to the reader to decide which ideas are worth exploring.

The articles, written by Dr Pierre Casse, Professor of Leadership at the Moscow School of Management SKOLKOVO, were published in *Business Leadership Review* (BLR) over the past 8 years under the title of 'Casse's Corner'. The objective was to reach out to stakeholders of the Association of MBAs (AMBA) and provide them with some commentary on what is happening in the leadership field at the beginning of this century. They were written with the idea of:

- Reviewing some of the key issues and challenges that leaders from both public and private sectors are facing today;
- Outlining what some successful leaders have been doing;
- Provoking readers out of their comfort zones and encouraging them to explore, if not participate in, the creation of new leadership trends.

Leading in the new world

"I want to put a dent in the universe"

- Steve Jobs

Today's fast changing world is not easy to understand. Leaders must face new and unexpected issues on a daily basis. In coping with the challenges they cannot simply use old solutions to solve new problems. It does not work that way. Some people are inventing a brand new world which is both exciting and scary. As a result, leaders are struggling with the need for both social and economic transformation without appropriate reference models.

Today's 'reset economy' demands the creation of new assumptions and values. If leaders are not up to the challenge of re-inventing these assumptions then mankind will experience a very painful process of regression. It has happened in the past and it can happen again. The new world we are in the process of creating requires leaders with new mindsets and styles. Some of the major challenges can be summarised as follows:

- Redefining the purpose of business;
- Rethinking the rules of the business game;
- Reflecting on the use of new technologies and their impact of the quality of life for millions of individuals;
- Fine tuning the interface between the private and public sectors;
- Inventing new organisations;
- Reviewing the way we look at people at work;
- And many more…

Learning from the new leaders

"Stay hungry, stay foolish"

- Steve Jobs

"Follow your inner moonlight, don't hide the madness"

- Allen Ginsberg

There are some leaders who are impacting the world in a very forceful way. Such leaders are inventing new ways of producing, selling and distributing goods and services and in so doing they are not afraid to break with the conventional approaches to leadership and management.

It is interesting to witness the co-existence of several distinct environments. For instance we can identify characteristics of what we might call the old economy, which are distinct from those of what we might call the new economy or the global economy. This multi-dimensional environment requires leaders who are both flexible and creative.

These new leaders are special in the sense that they do not come from the traditional educational systems such as universities, business schools, corporate academies and the like, but rather they emerge directly from the field. They are academic drop-outs without MBAs or PhDs. They are young and irreverent. They are dreamers with wild ideas and a unique flair for the unknown. This new breed of leaders believe that the best way to predict what will happen tomorrow is to invent it today and they act upon such beliefs. It is not that they can 'think outside the box' but that they have the ability to invent the new boxes and in many instances they go one step further and give the impression that they aim to live without boxes.

These articles aim at encouraging leaders to experiment with new ways of leading people. It is hoped that they will trigger some new thinking among team leaders and encourage them to stimulate some interesting discussion with their colleagues on a range of hot topics.

This approach will be characteristic of what leaders will be called upon to do in future, namely to establish environments in which people can perform in the best possible way and experience what we have called 'mind expansion'.

The validation of ideas

Most of the ideas presented in this book have been tested on leaders we have met while consulting or teaching. They led to fascinating discussions. We have learned a lot from the leaders' reactions and we have fine-tuned some of our ideas on the basis of their questions and comments.

From many confrontations with leadership practitioners, our key learnings can be summarised as follows:

1. Nothing must be taken for granted in the current phase of human development.
2. One key success factor for leaders is this ability and willingness to constantly check their assumptions and where appropriate, create new ones.

3. Assumptions are meaningless without the appropriate behaviours since it is what we do that makes all the difference.

Leadership assumptions: We are what we assume

"I have learned throughout my life as a composer chiefly through my mistakes and pursuits of false assumptions, not by my exposure to fonts of wisdom and knowledge"

- Igor Stravinsky

Some of the ideas presented in this book also aim at giving readers a chance to put their own assumptions into perspective and challenge their conventional ways of seeing things. We strongly suggest that readers look at the various articles and while doing so listen carefully to their emotional reactions while reading. Those emotions are important because they will inform the reader of their unconscious assumptions. By listening to their own feelings readers will learn something important about the way they construct their own reality.

Leading one's own mind requires three major abilities:

1. The ability to check our assumptions or subjective interpretations of what exists or happens: Are they working well?
2. The ability to challenge the existing assumptions: Are there other ways to see things that could be more effective?
3. The ability to invent the new assumptions: What about participating in the creation of reality through new explanations?

Leadership impact: It is what we do that counts!

This collection of articles does not try to propose any significant solutions but rather is geared at offering leaders an opportunity to explore potential alternatives to how they think and behave. If these articles can impact a leader's ways of feeling and behaving, so much the better as long as it leads to a positive and constructive outcome. This is why quite a few articles offer self-assessment exercises, or personal scorecards, designed to help leaders take stock of their profiles and decide on what they could do to improve their effectiveness by:

•   Building on their existing leadership strengths;
•   Reducing the impact of their weaknesses;
•   Discovering the potential talents which they possess but of which they

may not as yet be fully aware.

Many of the articles raise questions intended to channel the readers' thinking beyond the topics covered.

The book structure

The book has three main parts and a challenging conclusion.

Part 1 focuses on highlighting some of the major challenges which leaders are facing in a very turbulent and ambiguous environment which can give rise to many interesting opportunities. The world that is in the making at the beginning of this new century is both scary and exciting. It is scary because the lack of appropriate leadership could result in disaster for our societies. Leadership must be re-invented! The problems that have surfaced are not going to disappear on their own. Leaders in both public and private sectors must seize the opportunity and transform a complex and multifarious crisis into an opportunity for progress improvements in the quality of life in our societies.

Part 2 explores some of the current issues that corporate leaders are facing today. It is clear that there is a fundamental need to revisit the way in which people come together to invent, produce, sell and distribute products and services that can help as many people as possible to live a better quality of life. Leaders, with imagination and courage, must come up with new organisations that will more effectively leverage the brain power to which they have ready access. It is not an easy task, far from it. Nevertheless it is a critical necessity.

Part 3 examines the key leadership requirements which will ensure leaders have the wherewithal to perform and enjoy their roles in a fast-changing world. It addresses the need for the leaders to assess their strengths and weaknesses, challenge their existing assumptions and explore the need to transform some of their ways of thinking, feeling and behaving to meet the external and internal challenges.

The initial, and arguably the most critical challenge with which we are faced today is the need to create a new generation of leaders.

A new generation of leaders

Leaders must face it: part of their responsibility is to prepare the new generation of leaders. It is not an easy task, particularly when that means that the leader of today must:

1. Give up some of their power

    Why should they do this when they enjoy being in charge and getting all the benefits that power brings? Where is the motivation to let it go? Why should they help younger people to get ready to take their place?

2. Think long term and short term simultaneously

    This is quite a dilemma for which most leaders are not ready! They are under tremendous pressure to deliver short term results and yet they must also think about the future. Most of them have not been trained or educated to do this. This is new necessity that requires different mindsets and skills.

3. Train for the unknown

    It's a critical issue: How do you prepare the new generation for tomorrow when nobody has a clue of what tomorrow will require. What kind of skills should the new leaders acquire so that they can be actively and creatively engaged in the shaping the new world?

Tips for the readers

If we may, we would like to suggest that readers go through the collection of papers with the following ideas in mind:

*   Be selective: Do not read the papers in a sequential order. Pick up on the topics in which you are most interested. Keep in mind that real life is not necessarily sequential. Feel free to pick and choose at random.
*   Be critical: What is important is not so much what you read but what you think of what you have just read. Read with a critical mind. Stop from time to time and form your own ideas on the issues raised.
*   Be creative: Think about the following question: If I had had the opportunity to write something about this issue, what would I have said? Moreover, close the book and think about the kind of issues you would love to explore but which have not been raised in the book.

A final quote to conclude this introduction:

"It takes a great reader to make a great book"

- Orna Ross

Part 1:

The Business Leadership Challenges

Lost and alive! The challenge of doing business in a world that escapes our understanding

"The sound of sense"

- Robert Frost

"That must be wonderful; I have no idea of what it means"

- Albert Camus

"The business of art lies in this - to make that understood and felt which, in the form of an argument, might be incomprehensible and inaccessible"

- Leo Tolstoy

Introducing 'the ambiguity curse'

It seems that we humans survive by facing a world which is beyond our comprehension and understanding, taking risks and thriving on uncertainty. We live and grow despite the fact that:

- We don't understand what reality is all about: our comprehension (apprehension?) of reality is based on the assumptions (subjective interpretations) that we produce to explain what 'is'. Our world is a virtual one. We exist by trying to get as close as possible to reality. The ambiguity of the very world we live in is forcing us to make a permanent effort to understand it (including to understand ourselves since we are part of the world).

- We cannot convey to others our personal perceptions of the world: communication among human beings is also highly ambiguous. We must face the fact that we cannot understand each other. Nature has made us in such a way that our perceptions of the world are not only unique but also un-communicable to others.

- We are unable to predict the future: we make decisions without knowing for sure that they are sound and that they will deliver the expected results. We live and work with the illusion of controlling our destiny. We indeed exist in an uncertain and risky environment.

Acknowledging 'the ambiguity curse'

Ambiguity means that all things (people, situations etc.) are unclear, mean different things at the same time, are made up of contradictions and loaded with paradoxes. A good example of the ambiguity we experience every day is the fact that words are meaningless. Meanings are in people not in words. So here we are using the same words and meaning different things. This makes us both creative and hostile to each other (we are still killing each other for the sake of words).

Uncertainty is ambiguity in relation to the future and the unpredictability of our actions! This challenge is encouraging us to set up our own visions about tomorrow (what we would like to see in the future) and fight for it.

Actually, what is very interesting is to acknowledge the fact that nature has placed us into a 'foggy' world but has also given us the ability to cope with it, transform it and participate in its ongoing creation. We are partners in the evolution of reality; not just observers.

Understanding 'the ambiguity curse'

Research has shown that human beings have the ability to transform the ambiguity into something good for them. Here is a model that can summarise what we know about ambiguity and its impact on people's emotions and behaviours.

A three dimensional model on ambiguity

Dimension 1: Tension

Ambiguity is a source of tension. However one must realise that the tension is not necessarily negative. An environment that is low or flat on energy is not a good thing. Tension can be the trigger of new actions and lead to unexpected explorations as well as discoveries. One should also be aware of the fact different individuals can react quite differently when facing ambiguity. Research has also identified some major cultural differences regarding ambiguity; some people love it. Others cannot stand it; it depends on their cultural backgrounds.

Dimension 2: Frustration

Ambiguity can impact people's emotions and feelings in strong ways. Those feeling lost and not knowing what to do have a tendency to experience bad feelings and express some negative emotions: "This is wrong…I do not like it…I am wasting my time…Who did this…"
The frustration can be high especially if people value being on top of things, understanding the causes of what is occurring in their lives and being in charge of their own existence.

Dimension 3: Reactions

Human beings encountering ambiguity have three major ways to cope:

- *Withdrawing from the situation*: Sometimes the best way to make sense of an ambiguous situation is to get out of the 'box' (i.e. situation) and put things into perspective. It is true that sometimes we are too close to what is happening and therefore unable to make good sense of it. The challenge is not to withdraw forever and lose interest in the event - then it is more fleeing than withdrawing.

- *Taking initiative*: Ambiguity means in many cases that the door is open to trying a few (new) things. It is an opportunity for taking a risk and change the environment for the best. Here again, people are facing two major problematic issues i.e. to take unrealistic risk and fail on the one hand and to become overly aggressive on the other.

- *Analysing*: We can use our brain skills and study the situation we are in so that we understand why it is what it is. This is our best way to take stock and decide on how to move ahead and develop ourselves. The problem with this solution is that it sometimes leads to what we call 'Analysis Paralysis'. We analyse forever and never do anything (or do it when it is too late).

Tentative conclusion

We should keep in mind that ambiguity is also forcing us to improve our flexibility as well as our creativity. If what we are doing is not working, it is time to try something else. And if nothing we know is working, then we should start to be creative and invent new and adapted ways to cope and thrive [1] (e.g. 'Synectics' as a methodology using ambiguity to provoke the production of new ideas [2]).

Validation: the ambiguity test

Have a look at the three statements in the triangles hereunder and decide on what is wrong if anything! You see it now...? We really see what we want to see.

Questions

1. How do you attempt to deal with ambiguity in the workplace?
2. Can you describe a situation in which you used an ambiguous situation to your advantage (and / or to the advantage of your organisation)?

References

[1] Wilkinson D., (2006). *The ambiguity advantage: What great leaders are great at*, Palgrave Macmillan
[2] Gordon, W.J.J. (1961), *Synectics*, New York: Harper & Row.

The digital world and process leadership: Great opportunities in the making!

Introduction

"No matter how great we get with digital formats of instrumentation, nothing really quite duplicates the real thing"

- Michael Bolton

"Process leadership is the art of creating the proper environment so that people with bright ideas and energy can move ahead and contribute in the best possible way"

- Caine Learning Centre

There is no question that leadership is in a drastic transformation mode because of new technologies being invented, developed and used by people today. There is nothing unusual here; it has always been our way (the human way) to progress and develop ourselves i.e. through the creation and implementation of new technologies.

The digital world that we are getting into (which is still highly ambiguous for many people) requires new ways of leading and managing. We are again at a turning point in our evolution. There are three major opportunities offered by digital methods of communicating, working together and doing business:

1. A dramatic enhancement of our human creativity.
2. A major review (and transformation) of the roles played by our organisational leaders.
3. An ability (crucial for our survival) to face the new world leadership challenges.

Digital connections and creativity

The art of leadership is becoming more and more the art of transforming information into knowledge, making something meaningless into something meaningful for as many people as possible. The multiplication of rapid connections between various (and sometimes unexpected) sources of information is changing the way we promote and practice synergy. The use of various references (individual, social, cultural…digital) to look at the same situations we are facing enhances our creativity and innovation.

Digital leaders?

The power of knowledge is outgrowing the traditional patterns of authority in many organisations. Status and titles are increasingly replaced by the power of knowledge – or, even better, by the power to create knowledge. Those who master not only the invention of new technologies but also their expanding use are gathering the new power to direct and impose i.e. to lead!

The formal leaders (now often termed 'process leaders') are becoming more and more responsible for empowering those who seem to know more and better (the 'knowledge leaders'). It is a major shift in 'who is in charge'. The role of the process leader is to listen to what the knowledge people have to say and to do what they are told so that the right work is done in the right way.

Facing the digital challenges

> *"The hands of every clock are shears trimming us away scrap by scrap, and every time piece with a digital readout blinks us toward implosion"*

> - Dean Koontz

Our human world has evolved in dramatic ways during the last twenty years. The species is confronted with unusual and deadly challenges. It seems that the apparition of the new technologies is almost synchronised with the many societal and environmental problems we are facing (or is it in the reverse?). We can survive because we are producing new technologies. It is as if we were experiencing (without a clear will on our part) some kind of natural synchronicity!

The challenge of process leadership

> *"Recruit and employ people who are better than you are"*
>
> - Bill Gates

One of the most critical challenges for our process leaders is to align our new technologies (creating life, cloning, working on cell stems, working with people we will never see and know, using new drugs…) with our value systems. Leaders must help people to review and adapt what they think, feel and behave so that they are in line with the new technologies. The alternative is to be destroyed by the outcome of our own creativity! (Of course, this is not the first time in history that this process and challenge has occurred.)

Digital leadership?

The digital world is both challenging and scary. A new form of leadership is obviously required today. Here is a short self-assessment exercise which you can use to measure your readiness for the brand new world in the making.

Answer the following questions:

Question	Yes	No
Are you ready to admit that you do not understand what is happening in the world today?		
Can you easily say to people that you do not know?		
Do you see ignorance as a leadership plus?		
Can you trust what you do not understand?		
Do you realise that a mobile phone is a new way of being?		
Are you good at taking 'instructions' from the people who work 'for' you?		
Do you believe in reverse empowerment?		
Do you work for the integration of relevance?		
Is cloud computing exciting for you?		
Do you perceive cyber-crimes as a major threat?		

<u>De-briefing</u>

- *For seven 'yes' and more*: There is a good chance that you are ready for the digital world in the making and that you even enjoy its challenges.

- *For three to six 'yes'*: You are basically fine and yet struggling with the unknown (ambiguity) connected with the brand new 'brave world' we are getting into

- *For one to two 'yes'*: This is not your 'cup of tea'…or are you maybe already beyond the digital dimension of the world?

Closing comments

Leaders are back to the ultimate question: do we control the digital world and take advantage of it, or are we the 'slaves' of our own creation?

From strategic leadership to opportunity leadership

"Everything has been said but since nobody listened it is still good to repeat it"

- André Gide

Going with the wind

All the points made hereunder can be applied to two business trends (i.e. the green movement and the new corporate social responsibility drive).

They are around and it seems they are working very well. In other words they are both business opportunities and fundamentally good for us, human beings.

The power of hunches

In a fast changing world where everything is fussy and foggy, the old ways of planning ahead are not only obsolete but dangerous. Leaders today must lead not knowing what the challenges are and how to face them. They must give the direction despite their own confusion and doubt.

After all they are in charge.

There are basically three ways to look at strategic leadership in a turnaround world:

Model 1: Anticipate by guessing what the trends are going to be

Guessing is not perceived by many scholars and practitioners of leadership as serious and worth any attention. And yet…we have strong evidence that the use of intuition in business is absolutely critical for success. We know for instance that the ultimate step in a CEO's decision making is not based on facts and analysis but on hunches.

It is quite clear that successful leaders do have a special gift to spot in a given situation the emerging trends and to align their business operations to them despite the fact that there is no guarantee that it will work.

The anticipation is about what could be tomorrow! It is about gambling on what the people will enjoy tomorrow and be ready to invest in the new 'product'.

The key to success is to spot the emerging opportunities before anybody else.

A company that has been very successful at doing this is NOKIA. The CEO of NOKIA was able to spot the potential in the mobile phone business when a lot of people in the telecommunication industry still had some doubt about its future.

Another company that has been very good at doing this is Swarovski Crystal Company. It is amazing what it has accomplished for the last five years by just anticipating what the consumers will be interested in when they (the consumers) had no idea about it yet.

The motto is: Know what they want before they do!

Model 2: Build on others' successes by using a copycat strategy

Some leaders are smart enough to spot what is in the air. They watch those who are doing the right things in business and grasp very quickly what the new opportunities are.

They align themselves to the new trends by becoming (in a way) some kind of parasites feeding themselves on the investments and efforts of leading companies.

They go for the 'me too' strategy and just differentiate themselves by either adding some minor values to the product (or the service) or by building on their good names (brand).

Quite a few Japanese, Korean and now Chinese companies in the car industry have been extremely good at using the copycat strategy. They see what the big car corporations in Europe have been launching successfully and then... move on in with some new features presenting themselves as the state of the art technology.

The motto is: If they did it we can also do it!

<u>Model 3: Invent tomorrow today and create the new trends</u>

The great corporations are using a totally different approach. They create the trends. They invent products and services that people have never thought about. They are creative and innovative. They surprise customers with the unexpected. They go for the unknown.

The best example is, of course, Apple. Not only has it been extremely efficient in inventing new trends and impacting the industry in a totally unexpected way, but it has also transformed some industries (communication, media, music and video) in a 'wild' way.

Under Steve Jobs' leadership, Apple has been able not only to re-invent itself but also to force the competitors and the consumers to change their views and behaviours.

Apple is not afraid of trying out new things, exploring brand new avenues and competing against itself.

The Motto is: Let's be the best and…stay there

The opportunistic qualities

Do you as a leader qualify as an opportunistic business person? Just answer the ten following questions with yes or no.

Are you good at:

Question	Yes	No
Seeing what others do not see		
Guessing what could happen next when facing a challenge		
Being right in your predictions		
Turning mistakes into opportunities		
Spotting new trends before anybody else		
Being first with new ideas		
Enjoying ambiguity		
Pulling pieces together (quickly and effectively)		

Question	Yes	No
Taking risk		
Using flair to understand a given situation		

De-briefing

- *Between 7 and 10 'yes'* answers: You are an opportunistic leader! Be careful not to over trust your intuition.

- *Between 4 and 6 'yes'* answers: You have it but it can obviously be developed. Go back to the items you did not say yes to and reflect on what you could do to improve.

- *Between 1 and 3 'yes'* answers: Not your cup of tea. Well…nobody is perfect!

From crises to opportunities:
Let's stop blaming and start building

Each crisis is an opportunity

Leaders of the world must be aware - one way or another - that our human way to survive and grow on this planet is by transforming the major problems that we are facing into opportunities. Each major crisis that we have encountered since the beginning of time has been an opportunity for us to have a good look at our ways of living together, assess our strengths and weaknesses… and improve.

It is true that sometimes we did not take advantage of the crisis at hand; that we did fall into the traps of the time and unfortunately failed to progress. There is no fundamental difference with today's crises (financial, environmental, social etc.). They are giving us the chance to take stock, re-invent ourselves and move on with a better life for more people. Here are the three challenges the leaders of the world are facing today - the 'invisible hand' is giving us a chance to move forward again.

Taking stock

There is no question that we have transformed ourselves as well as our collective ways of living in drastic and sometimes totally unexpected ways during the last twenty years and it is not over. Actually we invent new possibilities of being more open and faster than ever before!

Consider, for example, the smart phone - it's much more than a phone… it's an alternative to our traditional patterns of thinking, feeling and behaving. The new technologies that we have invented and that we are now using have impacted us in many ways that we are not yet able to grasp and control. It seems that we are at the mercy of our own creativity and ingenuity.

Once more, however, we find that our technologies are advancing more rapidly than that our value systems - leading to confusion and ethical failures on a grand scale. We must catch up and align our value systems with the opportunities that our technological innovations are giving us on almost a daily basis.

Re-inventing ourselves

Each time our creativity has overwhelmed our social and cultural systems, leaders have emerged who have found ways of turning the new possibilities into something overall good for human kind... along with those who have exploited them for their own ends!

These leaders have not only understood the still obscured possibilities but they have had an ability to explain to others what they were and convinced them to try them out.

Today is not different. As in the past, we are facing the challenge of using our new discoveries in beneficial ways ... and to avoid being duped by those who seek to subvert progress.

Moving on

Do we have a choice? It seems that leaders have three major choices:

First choice: Deny the seriousness of the situation we are facing and basically patch up the problems with the old solutions (a bit reinforced and improved): "We are fine and everything will be alright. No need to change anything fundamentally and deeply."

We all know that won't do!

Second choice: Get cynical and caustic or criticise all the new inventions that are generated, steadily and forcefully. This attitude can lead to a dangerous valorisation of the past and rejection of new opportunities.

What a pity! What a risk to miss the opportunity and get into a major social and cultural regression. Ultimately this aggressive behaviour could destroy us.

Third choice: Analyse, understand and simplify the change so it can be channeled properly and used with a minimum of cleverness and wisdom - so as to enable the widest possible engagement.

This alternative is maybe the most difficult one. It requires a leadership based on the activation of our best cognitive skills as well as on a minimum of energy to change things around.

It is however what leaders did in the past (sometimes at the cost of their lives) with clear visions of what's in it for us living beings.

Leadership expectations

It is quite simple. What most people expect from their leaders (nothing new here compared to the past history) is:

- To have a global perspective and see the trends as well as the opportunities in the making.

- To have enough imagination to detect opportunities in the chaos of the current situations.

- To have courage and sell the new assumptions about ourselves and values about life to as many people as possible.

Of course it is not easy (who says that leadership is easy). Let's hope that some people will find a way to do it and save our future from our own tendency to shy away from uncertainty and adversity.

Are you that kind of leader?

Here is a little quiz to give you a chance to assess your leadership abilities to transform a problem (crisis?) into an opportunity (Just answer yes or no).

Do You:	Yes	No
Enjoy new challenges		
Like working on unexpected problems		
Know how to turn mistakes into opportunities		
Look at the positive side of a difficult situation		
Get excited when confronted with difficult questions		
Look for new paths to solve problems		
Rally other people around challenging projects		
Persist when others have already given up		
Search for alternatives when making decisions		
Search for new ways to do things		

<u>De-briefing</u>

- *If you have between 7 and 10 'yes' answers*: You are the kind of leader we need today. You will move forward … if you have the proper power to do so.
- *If you have between 4 and 6 'yes' answers*: It all depends on the situation you are in. You can do it if necessary. The potential is there.

- *If you have between 1 and 3 'yes' answers*: This is not your cup of tea. Your strengths are elsewhere.

Leadership and the power of the invisible hand

The invisible hand at work (Adam Smith – Emile Durkheim): the leadership issue

At this current stage in our evolution our collective lives are determined by forces that are beyond our grasp and control. Perhaps the day will come when we will be in full control of our own destiny, but let's face it, at this time, in all major dimensions of our lives we are determined, influenced and conditioned by natural drives over which we have no control - and in most cases little awareness. The current financial crisis and its impact is a good example of our incapacity to understand what is happening to us and control it (Adam Smith).[1]

It is becoming clearer to us that, by getting together at the same time and in the same space, we generate 'forces' which once we have created, predominantly through our communication processes, impact our very existence in the most fundamental ways. We are the slaves of our own social and cultural inventions (Emile Durkheim).[2]

There is a good chance that our main challenge in the 21st century will be related to the creation of tools that will enable us to begin to understand and control our social productions.

It is indeed time to learn how to produce what we want to produce and reduce our dependency on the invisible forces that have been driving us since the beginning of time.

The illusion of control

If you listen to any leader who is prepared to be open and speak candidly, he or she will tell you: "Frankly, I don't control much. Most of the decisions I make are more or less imposed upon me. I don't have many choices". If this is true, and I believe it is, then why the whole academic circus around decision-making and the power of making choices? It seems that human decision-making is pre-determined. It is like our economic systems: the invisible hand of Adam Smith is at work and influences us in such a way that we decide what we cannot decide! And, if we do, we then face major disasters and turmoil. We must go with the forces!

So here we are, leaders in search of certitudes that cannot be found anyway. We are suffering from the illusion of control. Therefore the proper conclusion is that leaders should:

1. **Know the forces** - learn how to identify the major moves of the invisible hand.

2. **Go with the forces** - Take advantage of those moves.

3. **Join the forces** - Be creative enough to join the sources of those moves and participate in the work of the invisible hand.

Knowing how the forces work

There are two critical processes which we can employ in order to detect the major trends both inside and outside an organisation; these are 'analytical search' and 'intuitive insights'. Overall, a combination of both is best because it provides a good cross-check and some validity to our conclusions.

The 'analytical search' approach – utilising facts and figures - can be successful as long as:

- You collect relevant and precise enough data.
  Leadership Key Question: Are you sure that you can trust the numbers that you are getting?

- Your analysis is thorough and complete.
  Leadership Key Question: Are you aware that most existing accounting systems do not provide a good basis for a thorough and solid analysis of what is really happening in your organisation?

- Your conclusions are challenged without any kind of restriction.
  Leadership Key Question: Do you know that most senior executives resent being challenged on their key ideas and conclusions especially by junior people or external experts?

The 'intuitive insight' approach is based more on our ability to use our natural flair to guess and have hunches.

I suggest that you quickly check your basic intuitive skills by answering the following ten questions.

Are you the kind of leader who:

Question	Yes	No
Knows that something is going to happen before anybody else		
Spots a winner (projects, people...) at first sight		
Has flair and can see where the wind is coming from		
Sees what other people do not see		
Can read people by just watching them		
Has difficulty convincing others of the correctness of your insights		
Identifies the hidden potential of a given situation		
Listens to clues		
Reads between the lines		
Has been proved right in his or her guesses a lot of times		

If you have a majority of 'no' answers then perhaps you should make sure that you:

- Are careful with your personal insights (so many people have had to suffer over the centuries because leaders have been wrong in their insights).
- Surround yourself with intuitive people and listen to them, at least from time to time.
- Develop your own intuition by practicing the art of 'Creative Intelligence'.

If you have a majority of 'yes' answers, perhaps you should:

- Check your insights especially when your decisions can impact a lot of people.
- Refrain from just going the intuitive way and cross-check your conclusions with some analysis.

- Give a chance to others to also express their gut feelings.

Going with the forces

Any marketing expert will tell you that the best marketing is no marketing at all. The second best is to sell to people what they want to buy anyway. In other words, the more you surf the wave the better off you are.

'Going with the forces' requires three major leadership abilities or talents:

1. A taste for the unknown- how good are you at facing ambiguity?

- Can you function well and be happy without knowing what the background of a situation is?
- Do you believe that an unclear situation can be the source of creativity and innovation?
- Are you able to be the source of ambiguity and to spread it around you?

2. A capacity for risk taking. We have no choice. We must go with the tide which means that we have to take risks. This requires courage. If there is no risk then there is no need for courage. How courageous are you? As a leader are you able to:

- Disagree with your manager despite the fact that you know that your action could jeopardise your career in the organisation?
- Speak up on behalf of one of your team members when you know that it is not quite politically correct to do so?
- Push a project that you feel strongly about when everybody around you is against it?

3. A pro-active flexibility - this is called 'agility' and it is characterised by the creation of a permanent 'learning how to learn' process that people experience in a continuous way. It is based on four critical abilities:

- The ability to discover. How good are you at taking stock of your environment and making a diagnosis of the forces that balance each other? (The 'Force Field Analysis' approach created by Lewin is a good technique [3])
- The ability to invent. How good are you at using your imagination and promoting new ideas? ('Synectics' by Gordon is a good way to achieve this [4])
- The ability to implement and adapt your action on the spot. How good are you at translating your great ideas into deeds and results? (The

very well known SCQA-Situation-Complications and Challenges-Questions- Answers- can be very helpful in this matter [5])

- The ability to learn from experience to avoid re-inventing the wheel. How good are you at learning from your own actions, getting good points out of your failures and building on your successes? (The 'triple A model - After Action Assessment' can be very effective in just doing that [6])

Joining the forces

The good news is that we are not completely at the hand of the forces. We belong to them. We are partners in the creation of reality. We participate in the creation and evolution of what determines our lives and future.

As such we can perhaps learn how to:

1. Initiate the creation of new forces.
2. Give some push to orient the forces already at work.
3. Maximise the positive side of what is happening anyway.

This is in a way the ultimate leadership challenge.

So perhaps we should add one name to our list of references: Adam Smith, Emile Durkheim and…….Charles Darwin!

References

---

[1] Smith, A. (1976), *An Inquiry into the Nature and Causes of the Wealth of Nations*, Chicago: University Of Chicago Press.
[2] Durkheim, E. (1957), *Professional Ethics and Civic Morals*, New York, NY: Routledge.
[3] Lewin K. (1951), *Field Theory in Social Science*, New York, NY: Harper and Row.
[4] Gordon, W.J.J. (1961), *Synectics*, New York: Harper & Row.
[5] See for example: Minto, B. (1996), *The Minto Pyramid Principle: Logic in Writing, Thinking, & Problem Solving*, London: Minto Books International, Inc.
[6] See for example: Ventrella, S.W. (2002), *The Power of Positive Thinking in Business: 10 Traits for Maximum Results*, New York, NY: Simon & Schuster.

Part 2:

The Corporate Leadership Challenges

An open letter to the non-leaders (who are very demanding, and rightly so)

Here are seven good reasons why you should not follow your leader! What do you think?

1) Your leader is manipulative

You know it and you resent it. You hate the feeling of being manipulated. The manager to whom you are reporting is using you for his own ends. Moreover he wants you to believe that he cares about you. He keeps telling you that you have a great future ahead, as long as you follow his orders. You cannot trust him.

Question: Do such people really exist?

<u>Three ways to recognise a manipulative leader</u>

Is your leader:

1. Asking you to do things for the sake of his own image?
2. Promising things to you but never delivering on his words?
3. Saying things to people (in front of you) that you know are not true?

2) Your leader is incompetent

It is so frustrating to realise that the manager you respected and even admired is incompetent. She does not know what she is talking about. She is not even aware of the mistakes she is making. She is wrong in so many cases and she blames it on others. To follow her means inevitable disaster.

Question: Have you ever worked for such a leader?

<u>Three ways to recognise an incompetent leader</u>

Is your leader:

1. Many times wrong in her diagnosis?
2. Unable to come up with some sound questions and potential answers?

3.   Always asking people what to do because she is obviously lost?

3) Your leader has no courage

What a disgrace to watch him bowing in front of other managers and keeping silent when you know that he should stand up and fight for the good ideas. What a shame to see that he is so shy in front of adversity and withdrawing from healthy confrontations

Question: It is so easy to criticise - do you have courage yourself?

Three ways to recognise a cowardly leader

Is your leader:

1.   Afraid of facing reality (especially bad news)?
2.   Being obsequious in front of senior managers?
3.   Praising people when they do not deserve it at all?

4) Your leader is a blocker

All your great ideas are rejected for unacceptable reasons: It is too late... We do not have time...We tried this before...It does not work here. Or even more frustrating: We need more information...Work on it a bit more...Let's check a few things first. All these are pretexts for no action. Your manager is addicted to procrastination.

Question: Can you by-pass such a leader?

Three ways to recognise a blocker leader

Is your leader:

1.   Always finding good reasons for not doing something?
2.   Allergic to change and very fond of status quo?
3.   Conservative and not quite in favour of innovation?

5) Your leader is a 'fake'

Let us face it, she does not have the right calibre. She must have been good in the past or in a previous position but right now she is a disaster. She does not have what is required to lead properly and effectively. She is lost and she wants to hide it. You could do her job. You could do even better.

Question: Could you really do better?

<u>Three ways to recognise a 'fake' leader</u>

Is your leader:

1. Good with words and weak with deeds?
2. Talking a lot about her glorious past?
3. Always volunteering for special projects and not delivering anything?

6) Your leader is too soft

You like him. Everybody does…but he is so weak. He is not able to say no. He cannot stand a conflict or a strong disagreement. He wants peace at any cost and the result is very messy. It has reached a point where his smiles and soft voice are irritating you and your colleagues. You cannot take it anymore. And yet he is so nice…

Question: Well at least he or she is nice. What else do you want?

<u>Three ways to recognise a soft leader</u>

Is your leader:

1. Spending a lot of time talking to people?
2. Using his charm to convince people to do something, but never forcing anyone?
3. Putting urgent projects on hold because some people are not comfortable with what's happening in the team?

7) Your leader is a sick 'star'

She inflicts pain on you and the other team members and she enjoys it tremendously. Yes, there is no question that she is brilliant and very successful. Her managers are always praising her for her great achievements. She is a star and yet she is 'sick'! To work with her is painful. She keeps showing you (and the team for that matter) that you are not up to her standards. She does not miss an opportunity to humiliate you in front of others and loves it when you fail.

Question: Do you think that you should get out of there?

<u>Three ways to recognise a sick star leader</u>

Is your leader:

1. So egocentric that it is always "me, I and myself"?
2. Not listening at all to other people's ideas but listening a lot to herself?
3. Pretending that there is no salvation without her. She is the one. The only one?

The question is obviously: What should you do if the leader you are working for belongs to one of the categories outlined above?

And, there is an important question here for the leaders too – do you see any of these traits above in yourself, and what can you do to change?

Well… I do have some answers (out of research and experience) but I would rather challenge you, the reader.

Discussion questions:

a) What is your own experience regarding the above leadership profiles?

b) Do they exist? Have you been confronted with one of them?

c) What have you done?

Leadership and boredom: Is there a lack of imagination in corporate leadership?

"Boredom: The state of being weary and restless through lack of interest"

- Merriam-Webster Dictionary

"The concept of boredom entails an inability to use up present moments in a personally fulfilling way"

- Wayne Dyer

There is something going on in many organisations and teams that is not only undermining performance but has also had a detrimental impact on the good spirit which should be characteristic of a healthy working environment. This malaise seems to be widespread and as far as we can see it is something which is not being addressed effectively.

To be more specific, it is a sad fact that many people are unhappy in their work and worse still, they are suffering from boredom, a condition which manifests itself in various forms. For example:

- Their energy level is very low
- Their days drag on and on and they are depressing
- They live for what will happen at the end of the day or when they finally get to the weekend

They simply suffer from the boredom syndrome!

Are your team members bored at work?

"Man finds nothing so intolerable as to be in a state of complete rest, without passion, without occupation, without diversion, without effort. Then he feels his nullity, loneliness, inadequacy, dependence, helplessness, emptiness"

- Blaise Pascal

It is truly amazing that people can spend a great majority of their time and life at work without getting any kind of great excitement from what they do. They may work long hours but are not satisfied with what they are asked to do. Many of them are just, plainly, irremediably bored. They survive and sadly have what we can call a 'small life'! Read the following statements from real people and decide if they apply to your team members:

- "I am ready for more at work but the job does not give me a fair chance to do it."
- "To be honest I am performing at 40% of my capacity."
- "Most of my brain skills are untapped."
- "Frankly my boss is not that exciting."
- "My co-workers are not so interesting."
- "I get my kicks after work when I leave the office."
- "What kills me at work is to see that others are enjoying good challenges."
- "I must drag myself to the office every morning."
- "Thank God, I have the computer and the internet at work."
- "It is so heavy at work that I sometimes get depressed."

More than five 'yes' responses should be analysed carefully and dealt with urgently because life is too short to be miserable! Boredom can mean that people are not living their lives to the full; that they are wasting it away; that they are in trouble. Your role as a leader (beyond the need to get good performance from your colleagues and team members) is to create an environment that is healthy and conductive to growth and development and, of course, good results. Current research shows clearly that happy people perform much better than people who feel miserable. It is not just an assumption without evidence. It is well proven.

Are you a boring leader?

"Boredom is the root of all evil...the despairing refusal to be oneself"

- Soren Kierkegaard

Boredom should get your attention if you are in a leadership position. There is no question that boredom at work is the sign of serious problems and the source of a dangerous disease. Leaders must be aware of the problem and use some good remedies. The first question any leader should be able to address is: am I boring? Is my leadership style and my way of managing and doing business such that it could be perceived as dull and de-motivating?

Have courage and dare to assess yourself by answering the following questions:

Do you:	Yes	No
Go to work full of excitement		
Challenge yourself all the time		
Love what's new and different		
Despise routine		
Like to explore new ideas		
Move (even physically speaking) at a high pace		
Have time for in depth discussions		
See work as more than a job		
Acknowledge that some people are smarter (even more intelligent) than you are		
Be creative under pressure		

De-briefing:

- *If you answer 'yes' to between seven and ten of the above*: You must be an exciting person to work with.

- *If you answer 'yes 'to between four and six of the above*: You can be sparkling at times but watch out for the 'routine' trap.

- *If you answer 'yes' to between one and three of the above*: Perhaps in some ways you are an effective leader but perhaps too you are a frightful bore.

What can you (as a leader) do to avoid it?

The tackling of the problem can be done according to (at least) three key actions:

1. **Assess the situation in your team: face reality with courage and imagination**

Do not assume that there is no problem, check and cross-check. Here is how you can do it:

- Have some feedback meetings to talk openly about the existence (or otherwise) of boredom within the team.
- Ask an independent outsider to come and watch the team at work and then report to you on his or her assessment (without being personal).
- Compare or benchmark with other teams and see if your team members are more or less passionate about what they do than other people.

2. **Decide on some motivating initiatives: create new ways to mobilise people's talents**

Be creative, redefine the work place, use imagination, create a free-from-fear environment, give space to people, encourage them to take initiative, empower. Here is how to do it:

- Redesign jobs so that there is a better match between people's expectations and the work requirements.
- Give special and exciting assignments to people from time to time.
- Take the team members with you to meet with senior executives and witness some important decision-making meetings.

3. **Invent a working place that goes beyond work and performance: innovate with your team members**

Get out of the box, invent the new way to get people happy at work and grow, be creative. Here is how to do it:

- Devote some of your meeting time to discuss non-job related issues that are exciting and relevant to people.
- Invite interesting people from outside the organisation to address life issues that people will connect with.
- Create a leadership rotation system so that different people will have a chance to lead the team from time to time (not just when you are away but also with you present).

Boredom is a disease

It is indeed a sickness and must be addressed as such. Good and healthy leaders know it and are not afraid to handle it. Are you such a leader?

And a challenging quote to conclude:

"Boredom: The desire for desires"

- Leo Tolstoy

From sensitive (sane) to brutal (toxic) leadership

According to our experience and observation, it is very rare to find people who have worked for, and with, outstanding, caring and effective leaders. Certainly they exist, but they are hard to find. If you are lucky enough to hook up with such a leader, then hang around and enjoy the experience. On the other hand, it is much easier to identify people who have had bad experiences with lousy, incompetent and at times, 'brutal' leaders. Such leaders are more in evidence.

Sensitive (sane) leadership

The first category of leaders we refer to as sensitive leaders. They lead with taste and are recognised by the fact that they are able to:

- Recruit people who are better than they are without feeling threatened;

- Create environments which are conducive to performance, joy, and people's growth; and

- Trust people and push them both forward and upward.

Brutal (toxic) leadership

Toxic leaders are those who use people for their own sake, manipulate them and build their reputation on other people's work and achievements. They use and abuse the power they have to promote themselves and eventually destroy others. They can be recognised by the following symptoms:

- They live on mistrust and lies;

- They talk down to the team members; and

- They create environments in which people feel bad, depressed, afraid and unhappy.

How sensitive is your leader? Go through the two questionnaires opposite (be as candid as possible, yes or no answers only) and assess these results in light of the following de-briefing:

Sane leadership: Leading with taste

Here are some of the main features of a great workplace:

- People enjoy working together. They smile and laugh. They cooperate, learn from each other, and if the competition is around it is perceived as being fair and a source of stimulation for all the parties involved.

- People are not hiding behind closed doors. They are open in discussions and you can feel that they are comfortable with challenging anybody, including the leader.

- Rumours are almost non-existent. People are direct in their communications. The power play is constructive and kept to a minimum.

Reflective question 1: What kind of leader do you have right now?

The person I report to:	Yes	No
Believes in me		
Gives me exciting and important assignments		
Puts me in the spotlight from time to time		
Ensures that I meet with important corporate people		
Encourages me to improve and expand		
Supports me when I take risks		
Provides all the support I need to perform well		
Fights for me (my promotions, recognition and rewards)		
Gives the proper public credit for a job well done		
Minimises the importance of my mistakes		
Challenges me so that I outperform myself		
Celebrates my successes on the spot		

Has great expectations regarding my future in the organisation		
Presents criticisms in a straightforward and caring way (with respect)		
Is more concerned about outputs than inputs		
Is flexible and tolerant		
Behaves as a positive role model		
Walks the talk		
Has credibility		
Has power and uses it with fairness and sensitivity		

De-briefing:

- *If you have between 15 and 20 'yes' answers*: You are lucky. Stay there. Enjoy as much as possible. Take full advantage of the fact that you have to work with a decent (sane) person who respects you and believes in you.

- *If you have between 8 and 14 'yes' answers*: Perhaps there is still some hope but we advise caution. See if you can influence your leader and eventually explore the possibility to coach him/her so that he/she becomes a better, more sensitive leader. However do not waste time. Start to check your options inside and outside your organisation.

- *If you have between 1 and 7 'yes' answers*: You may have a serious problem. You should move down to the next questionnaire!

Toxic leadership: Leading with distaste

How do you recognise a toxic leadership environment?

It is very easy to see it and it is dreadful! People are:

- Hiding from each other.

- Very cautious in meetings and basically going along with what they think the leader wants to hear.

- Lies are everywhere and mistrust is the norm.

Reflective question 2: How do you recognise a healthy leadership environment?

Please answer the following questions (as openly as possible).

The leader I report to:	Yes	No
Is over-ambitious for his own sake		
Uses power to move up the ladder		
Does not care much about his collaborators		
Spends a lot of time networking (and not performing)		
Blames you for his own mistakes		
Does not accept any kind of criticism		
Works behind closed doors		
Makes sure that you have a minimum of 'presence' in the organisation		
Exploits your own professional successes for his/her own benefit		
Minimizes the importance of your achievements		
Believes you should stay where you are and forget about moving up in the organisation		
Does not stand up on your behalf		
Does not keep you informed about what is happening in the team or organisation		
Spreads rumours and is very sensitive to gossip		
Likes to control you		
Does not face reality (especially bad news)		
Uses flattery with more senior executives		
Hides behind the bureaucracy to refuse well deserved recognition and rewards		
Plays one team member against another		
Is not credible		

<u>De-briefing</u>:

- *If you have between 15 and 20 'yes' answers:* Our advice is get out of there. This is toxic and dreadful. There is a high risk that in such an environment you lose your motivation, pride, and even worse your dignity.

- *If you have between 8 and 14 'yes' answers*: It is still bad and you must decide if you can help your leader change or not. Try a few things but give yourself some deadline. You cannot go on trying to influence your leader for too long - prepare yourself for a move out.

- *If you have got between 1 and 7 'yes' answers*: Perhaps there is some hope. Go back to the first questionnaire and see what could be done to improve the existing situation!

Conclusion

No perfect leader exists. However it is up to you to decide if you want to live somebody else's life or even worse, work with somebody who in the long run will make you (and maybe your family) sick. Keep in mind: it is one life, and it is yours!

Discussion

Were these reflective questions helpful and/or enlightening? If you are a leader yourself, has this exercise helped you to re-evaluate your own leadership style?

Power – The darker side of leadership

We are about to tackle perhaps the most critical issue in leadership: the acquisition and use of power in the corporate world.

Power is the name of the game. This is what leadership is all about! Or is it? I would like to raise three major leadership issues related to power and generate some reactions to my perhaps controversial claims:

- Politics (the power game that people play) is everywhere in the corporate world and is, in many cases, highly counter-productive.

- Power (at least as much as performance) is vital to a good career in any organisation.

- Power triggers cynical behaviours in quite a few people.

<u>1) The Power game and its leadership implications</u>

There is no question that as soon as people get together in the same place and at the same time the power game starts. Power is natural. It is also a requirement for professional effectiveness. You need it to perform well! What is the use of having brilliant ideas if you do not have the right power (authority) to implement them? The problem is that many young leaders do not know how to acquire and expand it. They are powerless and frustrated. They want to move but cannot do it. They do not know how to play the game. They are naïve in the power matter! Right?

<u>2) Power versus performance: the leadership dilemma</u>

Research (as well as practical experience) shows that the ability to associate yourself with people with clout is a must to climb the ladder in any organisation. In some cases it is more important than performance. This is called networking - to make sure the right people know the right things about you at the right time is critical for anybody's career. What is the use of being very effective if the people with power do not know it? Young leaders are basically… out of it! They do not invest enough time and energy in the 'game'. They think that to perform well is good enough to be recognised and promoted. They are mistaken. Is it not so?

<u>3) Power with a touch of leadership cynicism</u>

Face it! Nobody (well not many people anyway) is going to give you power without receiving something in return. Inexperienced leaders must learn that there are three major ways to get power and expand it beyond performance:

i) Your contributions to the bosses' ambitions and career.
ii) Your ability to be a nuisance to your boss and jeopardise his or her personal plans.
iii) Your ability to fake it and use flattery so that people feel good about you.

Discussion

Is this an accurate and realistic summary of the interplay between power and leadership? Are there other dimensions at work?

Managing creative workers - The new leadership challenge

Creative people at work

> *"Other people have brains too, you know!"*
>
> - Anonymous

The art of leadership in today's business world, more than ever before, is about creating the proper environment so that people can perform, use their talents to deliver great results and enjoy the opportunity and experience. Moreover, it seems that most great ideas no longer come from top executives but from the 'grass roots' of the organisation where those involved are well connected and in direct touch with trends in the market. These people are much more aware of reality on the ground and they have a better perception of what is required to stay ahead in the game.

One must also consider the old affirmation that happy people perform much better than unhappy ones[1] . The 'knowledge worker', a phrase first coined by business guru Peter Drucker some years ago, has now become the 'creative worker'. The new generation of people joining the corporate world want exciting jobs. These people want to contribute to the success of their organisations, grow on the job and enjoy the work they do. They also expect the proper recognition and reward for their efforts.

What's wrong with managing performance?

> *"Managing performance is still defined by many people as getting as much as possible out of people"*
>
> - Anonymous

The current notions around 'managing performance' are wrong and misleading. The concept is loaded with at least three major misconceptions:

1. People are still unable to manage themselves (Theory X).
2. Employees are followers and as such must have leaders to guide them.
3. People must be pressed to deliver outputs that the shareholders, the

market and the community expect (more is better).

However, effective creative leaders do not manage people's performance. They help people manage their own performance. This implies the following:

- In many cases people have an idea of what their contributions could be.

- People have the support and resources they need to achieve their objectives.

- The proper recognition and reward will be given to them at the end of their performance.

Research on motivation carried out by David McClelland[2] showed that most high performers like to set their own objectives, enjoy achieving them and work in the best possible way when they are under time pressure.

What's right with enjoying?

"Life is too short not to enjoy"

- Anonymous

The idea is very simple: Give people a chance to do what they are dying to do and the sky is the limit. This approach requires three simple and yet powerful leadership behaviours:

- Identify people's talents. Unfortunately so many organisational leaders are unaware of what their team members are really good at. In many cases, they are not even interested in knowing what their people's talents are.

- Give people a fair chance not only to use their talents but also to have enough space to stretch themselves and expand on the job - so many leaders are so preoccupied with the power game in the organisation that they forget that their first responsibility is to ensure the work is done properly and effectively. In this sense their team members too often become political assets at the expense of good work.

- Focus on people's strengths and forget about their weaknesses - So many organisations are wasting so much time, money and energy focusing on people's weaknesses instead of building on what they do well and enjoy doing.

Testing your leadership assumptions

Do you agree with the following statements?

1. Many managers focus so much on managing performance that they forget that those who do the work are real human beings with hearts, minds, hopes, dreams and aspirations.
2. The most important issue regarding performance and enjoying what you do is that most organisations prevent people from living their lives to the full.
3. Managers and leaders force people to live according to business criteria that are seldom in line with their individual aspirations or values.
4. What we are witnessing in many organisations is a process by which human beings are asked to think and behave against their own well-being.
5. Many value systems in organisations encourage managers to forget about their internal social responsibility.
6. Organisations suffer from the lack of human purpose and believe that business activities are more about agitations than progress in the quality of our lives.
7. People too readily surrender the right to live their own lives.

Can I suggest that you go back to the list, review your own reactions to each item and decide on what you could do differently to be a more creative leader?

References

[1] Drucker, P. (1957), *Landmarks of Tomorrow*, New York: Harper & Row.
[2] McClelland, D. (1961), *The Achieving Society*, Princeton: D Van Nostrand.

Facing the truth - Aren't we all corruptible?

"Corruption exists when an individual enters a transaction with the prevailing purpose of obtaining a personal benefit"

- Paul Claudel

"Corruption is the abuse of entrusted power for private gain"

- Transparency International

Defining corruption

Defining corruption is not an easy exercise. There has been a wide variety of definitions and many varied corrupt practices in various countries. Values and perceptions change. Corruption is a fact of life, something which is often difficult to accept.

In general, one can recognise that the concept of corruption encompasses a range of fundamental aspects such as decaying, turning bad, taking advantage of a situation in a hidden way, getting something that one really does not deserve, abusing the power that one has, cheating, and lying, to name but a few.

Are we all corruptible?

Our premise is as follows: nature has fashioned us in such a way that we are all subject to corruption at least to a certain point. It is just a question of circumstances and degree.

Let's face it: if corruption is the process by which an individual is looking for a special and personal advantage from a given situation, then obviously everyone is constantly open to the risk of being corrupted. Who is not looking for an opportunity to feel better and enhance his or her life? From time to time everyone is tempted to obtain unfair advantage from a given situation.

Whilst there is a type of corruption that doesn't hurt anyone, there is also a type that eats away at the very fabric of society. thereby rendering our lives difficult if not impossible. There is the type of corruption that takes advantage of a given social environment at people's expense. Although corruption is part of our collective lives, this doesn't mean it's acceptable.

Different types of corruption

At present people have a tendency to focus on one kind of corruption, i.e. the use of bribes to obtain an advantage from a situation, such as a good grade at university, an important contract for a business, a favour for a parent or a friend.

Here, we would like to focus on more subtle ways to experience corruption. We are talking about the following:

- *The corruption of the mind (the way we think)*
  This arises when we give up on our ideas to please somebody or to betray our deep convictions just to get a positive reaction from the people who have more power than we do.

- *The corruption of the heart (the way we feel)*
  When we play with other people's feelings to obtain personal satisfaction or when we are dishonest in the expression of our likes and dislikes to secure a good position within a social network.

- *The corruption of behaviour (the way we act)*
  When we do something to obtain an advantage where we know that it is not fair and that it will hurt people or when we cheat other people to maximize our personal advantage at their expense.

Measuring your corruption potential

The following exercise is aimed at giving you a chance to measure your predisposition to being corrupted. We dare you to test yourself.

Assess yourself on a scale from 1 (not me at all) to 10 (this is absolutely me):

How pre-disposed are you to:	Score
Changing your mind in discussion just to please the 'boss'	
Expressing feelings that deep down inside you do not have	
Saying things that go against your convictions	
Changing your position to follow the main trend in a group	
Doing things that you do not believe it	
Influencing others to get what you want from them	
Hiding facts that could hurt you	
Presenting yourself so that you are to your advantage	
Showing affection when other people do not resent anything	
Exploiting a situation to your interest	
Misleading people so that you look good	
Congratulating people when they do not deserve it	
Trying to get a benefit out of other people's actions	
Pretending and bluffing	
Accepting compliments which are undeserved	
Acting a part instead of being authentic	
Manipulating facts so that you look good	
Avoiding situations that can penalise you	
Using power for your own sake	
Making sure that people follow you blindly	

De-briefing

- *For a score between 20 and 50*: Congratulations – it seems that you are quite strong at resisting the temptations of corruption and that you know where to draw the line. But are you sure that it is indeed the real you or rather the person you would like to be?

- *For a score between 51 and 70*: Welcome to the real world of truly human beings. We are all open to some kind of corruption – at least from time to time. It is called survival. I suggest that you go back to those items that you scored quite highly on and see what you should be more careful with.

- *For a score between 71 and 100*: Something must be wrong somewhere! Either it cannot be so bad or you have lost your soul in the process of interacting with other human beings.

A final question

Reflect on the following quote from Sophocles:

"Truly, to tell lies is not honorourable; but when the truth entails tremendous ruin, to speak dishonourably is pardonable."

From dreams to nightmares - The faux pas of well-meaning leaders

Sad news

"A vision is a dream with a deadline"

- Anita Roddick

My experience as a consultant over the last ten years has led me to the following conclusions regarding top level leadership in both the private and public sectors:

- Beautiful and exciting dreams are not pre-conditions for success in the organisational world.

- The more inspiring the dream, the more disappointed people become when it fails to be realised.

- There is nothing worse than having mobilised the forces of an organisation or country around a powerful and promising scheme then have to inform people later that the vision is no longer appropriate and as such must be abandoned.

It is sad to see a valid and motivating dream fall through. It may happen for many reasons, three of which are particularly important:

1. The dream is grandiose but the implementation is faulty

   This is a common occurrence. The idea is very good and makes sense but the translation of the idea into concrete results proves problematic. Priorities have not been properly identified and too many targets are being pursued at the same time. There is dilution of energy and a dispersion of effort. This quickly leads to frustration and disappointment. Furthermore, should doubts arise regarding the relevance of the dream, the success of the plan will be jeopardised.

2. The quality and effectiveness of communication is poor

   It is amazing to see that many top executives believe that once they have articulated the dream, prepared a flyer for circulation and disseminated it on the intranet; everything is clear, understood and people are committed. Unfortunately nothing could be further from reality. A new dream must be constantly repeated, presented, articulated and illustrated. The dream of one does not automatically become the dream of many. On the contrary, it requires dedicated effort by the leader to sell the vision.

3. Top executives are often too impatient

Many leaders, particularly those with great ideas about the future, can become very impatient with people who apparently do not grasp the value of their vision, are too resistant to change and much too slow in the implementation of the plan. This impatience leads to more ambiguous signals from the top and less engagement down in the organisation. It can even trigger a major disruption in the organisation with each party blaming the other for the apparent failure of the dream.

The impact of a failed dream

The result of having a beautiful dream which fails can be catastrophic for an organisation or country. It can lead to:

• Frustration at the top where negative value judgments are formed of those people who 'fail' to implement the great ideas. In some cases it will go as far as declaring the people 'down there' as incompetent and not up to the challenge ("the dream is too good for them").

• Resentment among the company doers who complain about top leaders' unrealistic expectations and their lack of support. Very quickly people then start to question the credibility of their senior executives ("they do not know what they want").

• Consternation amongst people outside of the company who cannot believe that such a promising vision disintegrated and proved untenable.

A case in point

This is the real story of a very successful French company actively involved in communication, energy and transportation. Market leader for a while, the company lost its CEO who was then replaced by another who was ambitious, a visionary and new to the company. The incoming CEO came up with an inspiring vision that he presented as follows: "Let's become a high speed company".

A communications strategy was then designed around how best to impact the company's customers, stimulate new business opportunities and mobilise staff. The action towards the customers went very well. The one geared at selling the new vision to the employees did not work at all despite all the communication tools used i.e. pamphlets, videos and intranet.

Many people in charge of the transformation of the company kept both praising the new vision and complaining about the lack of a realistic plan for its implementation (too many unrealistic targets decided upon too fast, inadequate structure for good execution, lack of the proper means and resources etc.). But the main criticism from the managers and employees was the lack of direct, face to face, contact with the CEO and his top team. They felt that they had been left to themselves.

Six months after the launch of the new vision, the CEO, out of frustration with his own staff and pressure from the stock market, decided to go back to 'business as usual'. The result was catastrophic. The CEO lost his credibility, the managers and employees lost their determination and the customers lost their trust. The organisation went down in an inexorable way.

Leadership learning

The learning from research and experiences is quite simple:

1. As a leader you must have an idea of where you want to be with your team, organisation or even your country in the future. You must have a vision, (a dream), that should be easy to understand as well as inspiring and loaded with emotions.

2. It is absolutely vital to translate the dream into a step by step plan so that its translation into actions is managed properly. This requires the following leadership musts:

•   The decision regarding the top priorities (what should come first);

•   The selection of the key people who will be responsible for the implementation of the key decisions that have been decided upon;

•   The allocation of the proper resources so that the change agents have everything they need to perform well and achieve their objectives.

3. All business, corporate and political dreams require some adjustments during execution. The leader must be ready to adapt and change parts of the plan during its execution. No plan is adaptation free. So a regular check on the part of the top leaders is also mandatory so that the proper fine tunings is done at the right time.

Without those three key actions, the dream risks becoming a nightmare!

Three questions for the readers

1. Do you agree with the main points presented in the paper?

2. Do you have a dream for yourself? Your team? Your organisation? Your family?

3. How clear are you regarding how you are going to make it happen?

Leadership hypocrisies:
The lies that kill trust

The issue

"Hypocrisy is a fashionable vice and all fashionable vices pass for virtue"

- Moliere

Lets' be clear from the outset: leaders have no choice! In order to survive and function properly they must present the 'truth' in such a way that people will accept it. This approach is often referred to as 'Communication Cosmetic' or in other words, 'lies'.

This process is fine so long as:

- The lies do not go too far and do not twist reality in such a way that decisions and actions can be jeopardized by them.

- The leaders are aware of what they are doing and do not believe their lies.

- People are not damaged by the process of manipulating communication.

Moliere captured the heart of the issue very well: Telling everybody the truth can prove a major blunder in a social context. We need the 'cosmetic' approach. Lying is part of human nature and without it we wouldn't be who we are. But for me personally, there is one type of lie that is totally unacceptable. Leaders must never be 'hypocrites'.

Lies versus hypocrisies

"A learned fool is more than an ignorant fool"

- Moliere

Hypocrisies are lies which are intended to mislead people into believing that the liar holds a desirable and revered attitude. Each hypocrisy is an incorrect assumption presented to other people as if it was a representation of sincerity. The hypocritical leader uses lies with the voluntary intention to induce people into believing they stand for something which they do not. This is a very dangerous behaviour which can backfire irrevocably once people become aware of the manipulation to which they have been subjected. It destroys trust permanently. No *a posteriori* justification can repair the damage done. The research on the issue is clear: trust is not so easy to build and yet can be destroyed so very quickly.

It is amazing to see that so many organisational leaders fall into the trap of using that conscious way to manipulate others. They know that what they are saying is not true and yet they do it for the sake of:

- Looking good

- Getting people's support

- Pleasing their managers

So it seems that the habit is closely connected with power game that people play in all organisations. Hypocrisies can have a very negative impact on:

- The leaders themselves

- The people who are working with leaders

- The organisation itself

Are you a hypocrite leader?

Do you ... (Yes or No)?	Yes	No
Hide things from people to protect yourself		
Avoid sharing information on purpose		
Keep sensitive knowledge to yourself		
Suspect others of lying to you		
Manipulate information to your advantage		
Enjoy playing the power game		

Do you ... (Yes or No)?	Yes	No
Contradict yourself when necessary		
Not believe in the truth (anyway)		
Say one thing and do something different		
Talk behind people's backs		
Retain information when you think it's necessary		
Avoid answering direct questions		
Believe that it is all about politics in the corporate world		
Change your position according to the situations that you are in		
Blame others for your own mistakes		
Say things that you know are not true		
Take sides when appropriate for your own sake		
Look very candidly when misleading people		
Align your position with the powerful people to serve yourself		
Not stand up for people who are right and in trouble		

<u>De-briefing</u>

Look at your 'yes' and 'no' and assess yourself on the following scale:

- *For 1 -4 'yes' answers - Can sometimes act mistakenly*: There are times when we mislead people subconciously or involuntarily. In other words, we lie in 'good faith'.

- *For 5 - 9 'yes' answers - Can lie from time to time*: There are situations that are not easy to handle and to speak the truth can be damaging and harming. Leaders must sometimes be careful in being too transparent. The truth is very important but the timing, the way it is shared and the selection of the target audience can be very critical.

- *For 10 or more 'yes' answers: Can behave as a hypocrit:* Now this is not good. To lie on purpose knowing what we are doing (as leaders) can be very damaging for the people around as well as for the leaders themselves. Many organisations are plainly sick because their leaders are not honest enough. They lie on purpose and...lose their souls in the process.

Leadership guidelines for the hypocrite leaders

> *"I have the defect of being more sincere than persons wish"*

> - Moliere

Here are three basic leadership guidelines that well-meaning leaders can use to make their environments healthier:

1. Be aware of what you are doing.

2. Realise the danger of being a hypocrite and know that it can be very destructive.

3. Manage your 'lies' so that they do not go too far. Remain ehtical.

Injustice: The poison that undermines corporate performance and destroys people

"Injustice anywhere is a threat to justice everywhere"

- Martin Luther King Jr

"There may be times when we are powerless to prevent injustice, but there must never be a time when we fail to protest"

- Elie Wiesel

"As long as justice and injustice have not terminated their ever renewing fight for ascendancy in the affairs of mankind, human beings must be willing, when needed, to do battle for the one against the other"

- John Stuart Mill

Justice

Most normal, healthy human beings are imbued with a sense of justice and fair-play. As we interact with each other in our daily routine, we expect to be treated with transparency, equality and fairness and we realise that those around us expect the same in return. This predilection for justice is an expectation that must not be ignored in the organisational world.

This need for justice and the respect with which we give it in our mutual interactions is an importance characteristic which has evolved with our species. As animals, coping with the demands of an often hostile environment, we have learned that survival requires that we collaborate. The important issue in collaboration is reciprocity. We have come to realise that "one good turn deserves another". In other words, as I help you, so I can legitimately expect you to help me. We interact in this way because it is in our mutual interest to do so.

It is difficult to imagine how life could progress without this innate sense of justice. Mutual trust would be impossible and without a modicum of trust, effective collaboration could not happen. As distinct, unique individuals we cannot survive in isolation. Through our evolution we have learned that we need each other but for the relationship to work to our mutual benefit, we must satisfy our expectations for justice and fair-play.

Transparency

The importance of transparency in managing relationships within the organisation is too often underestimated by corporate leaders at every level. Nowhere is this more evident than in the assessment of performance, particularly at the level of the individual. Many people have little or no idea of the criteria their organisational leaders use to determine the quality and effectiveness of what they do. As a result individuals are at a considerable disadvantage in trying to manage their career aspirations and plans. They find themselves in the uncomfortable position of knowing they are under scrutiny whilst not knowing by whom and for what. It seems inevitable that feelings of resentment and unfairness will result and morale will deteriorate. The contagion can so easily spiral out of control all the while being totally unnecessary and easily avoided.

For the individual, critical and recurrent questions include:

What does the organisation expect of me in terms of performance?

Of course the organisation must have expectations of every employee at every level and such expectations must be in line with what the organisation is trying to achieve. However, often a distinction can be made between what the organisation as a whole expects and what the individual leader expects both in terms of end goals and performance goals.

How am I going to be judged?

If organisational expectations of each individual are to be met and those responsible for ensuring high levels of performance are to ensure that people are meeting the standards, then people must know what those standards are and how they will be assessed accordingly.

What's in it for me?

All too often, organisational leaders forget that ensuring expectations are met is a two-way street. People have a right to know that if they meet the standards in terms of expected performance, then there will be recognition and reward. Performance norms are impotent without related incentives and both must be clear to everybody.

Many such questions related to a lack of transparency in organisations remain unanswered and so people have little choice but to speculate on possible answers or ignore such questions altogether and hope for the best. A lack of transparency can prove poisonous in any organisation.

Equality

> *"A kingdom founded on injustice never lasts"*
>
> - Seneca

People want reassurances that they are working on a level laying-field with respect to others in the team/organisation. If such reassurances are not forthcoming, then morale can deteriorate rapidly. However, sometimes, differences in performance standards may be necessary. For example, if a particular project is critical to the survival of the company and performance expectations are higher than expected elsewhere in the organisation, then differences in expected norms may be justified. However, if standards in performance expectation and assessment are variable at the level of individual/team in the organisation, the justification for such variability must be explained.

The need for underlining the importance of equality is often overlooked. There is little evidence that organisations are places where life is equitable, and people are treated similarly. This can give rise to a deepening malaise, symptoms of which can include:

- Senior executive s and others the further you move up the food chain are treated according to status. The higher up the hierarchy you go the more lavish the treatment. However, people further down the food chain are told that times are tough and belts must be tightened. The inconsistency is difficult to understand.

- Those in the organisation who have the right connections seem to benefit irrespective of performance and the reasons are unclear.

- The political game generates feelings of inequality since those who play the game effectively seem to benefit over those who concentrate more on performance improvement. As a result, particularly when mistakes are made, some fare better than others.

Many women complain that corporate systems are not based on equality, (see the contrast between remunerations between men and women for the same jobs). A Lack of equality is corruption.

Fairness

"Anger may be foolish and absurd, and one may be irritated when in the wrong; but a man never feels outrage unless in some respect he is at bottom right"

- Victor Hugo

A sense of fairness is essential if a positive stable environment is to be established and maintained. There must be consistency in recognizing and rewarding desirable behaviors as well as sanctioning behavior which is undesirable. People are very sensitive to the following issues:

- You (the manager)made a promise to me and you are not keeping your word;

- Favoritism is by definition unfair and destructive of trust;

- The assessment of my performance is biased and not factual.

A lack of fairness is depression.

The consequences of injustice

"If thou suffer injustice, console thyself, the true unhappiness is in doing it"

- Democritus

Experience has shown that the expectation for justice in many teams and organisations is being consistently ignored and left unmet. As a result, people fail to perform to their true potential and the level of toxicity in the human system increases gradually over time. The consequences can be extremely traumatic at every level and can ultimately lead to the demise of the organisation itself. It is worth considering the impact of injustice at three different levels:

Organisation

At the level of the organisation, injustice is like a contagion, a virus which if left untreated spreads out to infect every aspect of the environment. This sickness can ultimately prove terminal. A lack of trust mushrooms as politics takes precedence over collaboration and meeting objectives. The organisation's reputation beyond its boundaries is adversely affected. The deterioration in reputation further fuels morale and those within the organisation disengage and show reluctance to commit.

Team

Maintaining a positive and vibrant team spirit is impossible if there is a sense of unfairness within the team. Team members begin to question the team leader's motives and play the political game for self interest rather than focus on ensuring team performance. Conflicts arise which sap the energy within the team and gradually all cohesion is lost.

Individual

At the level of the individual, injustice can have a particularly detrimental effect on star performers within the team. When rewards and recognition are not fairly distributed according to performance and results achieved, outstanding performers can quickly become demotivated. Under such circumstances, top performers disengage and look to invest their talents elsewhere. Individual performance deteriorates, teams underperform and the organisation suffers as whole.

The 'rights' of injustice

"Injustice in the end produces independence"

\- Voltaire

However, perhaps there can be something good to be derived from injustice. On reflection, we can see at least three major positive justifications for it:

1. It stimulates people into action and forces them to address a situation which has become unacceptable.
2. It gives people an opportunity to stand up for what they believe is right.
3. It can be a source of questioning and the starting point for a major

change process in a team or organisation.

Nevertheless, where injustice exists, leaders must recognise the fact and take steps to address the impact if it is to lead to something positive.

Testing your justice sensitivity

Using the following scale as a guide, please assess yourself for each of the items listed hereunder.

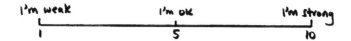

By and large I...	Score
Resent being ignored in meetings	
Cannot stand favoritism	
Value frankness	
Challenge biased rules	
Try to be straightforward with other people	
Believe in fairness for all	
Stand up for others	
Resent the power game people play	
Cannot stand corruption	
Enjoy working with people who are outspoken	
Believe that justice and trust go together	
Have a major problem with unfairness	
Think that everybody should be treated the same way	
Am convinced that systems should serve people (not the reverse)	

Appreciate knowing what organisation's key performance indicators are	
Share information (however sensitive) with everybody	
Resent clans and intrigue	
Fight for justice within my team	
Walk the talk and try to be as just as possible	
Do not lie to people	
Total score	

De-briefing

- *If your total score is between 20 and 70*: It seems that you are not really concerned about the issue of injustice. It could be good for you to look around and benchmark your attitudes and behaviours against others, particularly with respect to the issue of injustice and its impact on the individual, team and organization. Are you really insensitive to the issue of injustice or is it that you are afraid of the challenge?

- *If your score is between 71 and 150*: You are wise enough to consider the importance of injustice in the corporate world and apparently you are already making some good moves to ensure that people feel they are treated fairly and justly. It could be useful to review where you have assessed yourself high and low and examine how you can build further on your strengths and address some of your weaknesses.

- *If your score is between 151 and 200*: If this high score is a true and honest reflection of how you would assess yourself, then you are overdoing it. It is vital to develop an environment in which a sense of justice predominates but let's face it there will be time when fairness and equality cannot be ensured and for some legitimate reasons i.e. the success of the company, the pressure from the competition, the well-being of the majority and even, in some cases, some legal requirements. We suggest that you revisit all your scores and check on their validity.

Conclusion

A sense of justice is something which has always been characteristic of human communities. It is part of our biological make-up and potential. The main issue with respect to injustice is threefold:

- The concept and its related values are culturally subjective and individually biased.

- Power plays a very important role in determining what justice should be and who should be entitled to what, in the various social games that people play.

- The practice of fairness and justice require particular leadership traits, (as described in the article), that are not easy to find in the world around us.

A tentative conclusion and one which is put forward with an open mind can be reflected in the words of famous author Harpcr Lee:

> *"…but before I can live with other folks I have got to live with myself. The one thing that doesn't abide by majority rule is a person's conscience"*

> - Harper Lee, *To Kill a Mockingbird*

Part 3:

The Profiles of Leaders

Who needs leaders?

I would like to challenge you around one simple and yet, I think, very relevant question: *"Do we really need leaders?"*

After more than twenty years' experience working with many leaders from a wide variety of corporations across many industries, it seems to me that in many cases people would be better off without their leaders.

I have seen at least three major issues related to the misuse of power by company leaders at all levels and across all functions. I challenge the readers to react to my propositions and prove me to be either wrong or simply over-stating the point:

1. Many people perform not for the sake of the business but essentially for the sake of their leaders' personal ambitions.

   A lot of people in the corporate world complain about the fact that they spend more time and energy on working to please the 'boss' rather than on delivering good business outputs. As a result, they feel manipulated, and in many cases, powerless. The system supports this kind of hypocrisy. The main idea behind the leader's behaviour can be summed up as follows – "you serve me and perhaps there maybe a chance that I will help you later on!"

   I challenge the reader to tell me that this 'sickness' does not exist!

2. Many people start to outperform themselves when their leaders are away.

   It is in a way amazing to witness the transformation that affects people when their leaders are not around to give them instructions and micro-manage them. The team leader has barely left and team members start to feel more relaxed and able to take the initiative on their own. It is as if suddenly they are free to function as they would like and perform better. They enjoy not being controlled and constrained. They are now in charge...

   Would the reader share this perception with me or not?

3. Many leaders have a difficult time with brilliant people.

It is a fact that brilliant people are not easy to understand and manage. In actual fact, they do not want to be managed. They are at their best when they feel independent and autonomous. Leaders have major difficulties in handling 'stars' and outstanding performers. They are not so good at creating a working environment in which outstanding people can contribute in the best possible way. Many great contributors have learned the hard way that "if you are brilliant, better to hide it"!

I am sure that many readers can think of such a person who has been misunderstood and ostracised by his or her leader. Am I right?

My conclusion is that there is something basically wrong with many leaders and their ways of dealing with their partners in the organisational world.

Many people want to perform well, enjoy their work and grow on the job. The paradox is that on the one hand the system (through leadership) is asking them to be productive and on the other hand it is creating a lot of obstacles that prevent them from expressing their true potential. Something is wrong!

Once again, I challenge you, the reader, to tell me why we are supposed to spend so much time in such schizophrenic environments?

If I dare push the issue a bit further, I would go so far as claiming that a lot of men and women have indeed across time suffered tremendously from the unacceptable dreams of some 'sick' leaders. How many people throughout history had to die for the sake of a few mad leaders?

Having said that I must admit that there is a new trend in evidence – we are getting close to a time when leaders will be accountable not only for their business results but also for the sanity of their corporate partners. But is this really the right way to go? Don't you think that each individual should be responsible for his or her own mental health and life?

Who would want to be a leader?

Who, in his or her right mind, would want to be a leader today? Who would want to be in that awkward position of being responsible without having the proper power to do what's necessary to succeed? Who is ready to face all those new challenges with which nobody feels quite comfortable?

Let's face it - to be a leader in today's world is not only challenging but also scary. On top of it you have all the pain but without much compensation. So, it hardly seems worth it anymore. I can see three major issues with which leaders must cope:

1.   Leading in the fog

Most leaders are lost! Although some of them know and accept it, most do not want to acknowledge their confusion and anxiety. They try to bluff their way out and the cost can be very high.

Either way, leaders must still lead despite the fact that they do not know where they are going, and even if they do have some vague idea, they do not know how to get there. Furthermore, they have little idea of what might happen as a result of what they do, the consequences of which invariably are irreversible.

One must admit that to understand what's happening (and why it is happening) is almost impossible. There are too may things happening simultaneously. The world is becoming even more unpredictable and we are all prone to mistakes. Moreover, if we add the need for leaders to explain (clearly and effectively) to others what's happening while being totally confused themselves, we comprehend that to want to be a leader is pure madness.

Question to the reader

Do the above paragraphs ring a bell? Isn't it true that to lead without a minimum of certitude can indeed be an ordeal for most people?

2. Leading from the back

The time when the leader was out in front, leading the charge, is over. Now the leader is supposed to be in the middle or even in the back. Gone is the prestige of the role. Gone is the gratification attached to the leadership function. Gone is the applause that so many leaders expected and enjoyed in the past. Gone is the glory.

What remains is the hard work of making others successful. In most situations leaders no longer have any power. In fact many leaders have to beg people to do things. They have to persuade others of the validity of their views and decisions. They can no longer impose anything. They are progressively becoming 'servant leaders'.

In fact what we are witnessing is that in an increasing number of corporate situations people are instructing their leaders in what they must do in order that they, the team members, can perform well. A world upside down.

Question to the reader

Who wants to be a servant leader?

3. Leading with no trust

One major problem that leaders cannot ignore nowadays is that they can neither trust the people who are reporting to them nor the information, (including the numbers), they are given. What an insecure position!

Nevertheless, a leader still has to decide and move forward despite the fact that they can not be certain as to the accuracy of the data upon which they base their decisions. They must assume that the information they are receiving is right and accurate. They must assume that their partners in business know what they are talking about. They must assume that the situation has not evolved since the last exchange. There are a lot of assumptions!

Even worse, in many cases leaders are not quite sure that they can trust themselves: Are they really up to the challenge? Can they really pull this one off? Can they lead in such conditions?

Question to the reader

What do you think leaders should (could) do to improve the situation? Can you make three concrete suggestions that effective leaders could implement to enhance their leadership performance?

It seems that this is only scratching the surface of the evolving leadership concept and persona. Actually leadership is in the process of being completely reviewed and revisited.

What do people expect from their leaders in the time of crisis?
Answer: The very best!

An unpredictable world

> *"Most of our political elite has not realised that the world is flat"*
>
> - T. Friedman

Let's face it – many people feel totally lost when they confront the kind of situation we are in today: a turnaround world full of uncertainties! Not only do people feel lost but they also get frustrated and scared…who knows what could happen next? This world in the making is so unpredictable.

A natural reaction of men and women facing ambiguity (apparently since the beginning of time) is to look up to their leaders and get some guidance from them: *"That man Moses led us out of Egypt, but now we don't know what has happened to him. Make us a god and lead us."* (Exodus 32:23)

They ask their leaders to tell them how they can survive in this wild world. So, first let's take a look at what people do not want to get from their leaders in a turbulent time, i.e. today. And then let's examine the real expectations of people when it comes to leadership in a crisis.

The misery of bad leadership

> *Bad leaders…"rob people of their pride and dignity".*
>
> - Jim Adamson

Sometimes you wonder what is happening in some leaders' brains. In the past few years we have already witnessed nearly everything you can find in the book of 'Don'ts'. People are shocked when they all of a sudden see their 'great' leaders:

- Withdrawing from their people and being silent
  They have disappeared. They are hiding somewhere hoping that the problem will fade away on its own. They are not around anymore. They

79

have vanished. They have nothing to say.

- Lying to people and making false promises
  They face people with a smile and explain that the situation is not so bad and that everything is under control. You can then wonder why they are selling their stocks and activating their famous 'golden parachutes'.

- Sending conflicting signals and creating even more confusion
  They communicate in such a way that everybody becomes even more lost. The messages are not consistent and the delivery is ambiguous at best.

- Saying one thing and doing quite the opposite
  They talk about cost cutting in a very powerful and convincing way to the people, but then they do not walk their own talk and spend money on a 'nice to have' item.

- Behaving in an inconsistent way
  They launch a strategy and change it after a short while. They keep switching from one priority to another and by doing so they trigger an enormous frustration among people who care for the survival of the business.

All of the above behaviours (and many more not listed here) are extremely counterproductive. They demobilise people and make them sceptical, or even worse – cynical.

Here is a simple questionnaire to gauge how the above mentioned points relate to your situation:

Leadership learning questionnaire 1

The leader I report to:	Yes	No
Avoids communication with staff		
Answers straightforward questions in an ambiguous way		
Asks senior executives to handle sensitive issues on their behalf		
Does not take control in a difficult time		

Does not face up to reality		
By inertia hopes for a better situation in the middle of a tough time		
Delays taking pressing decisions		
Blames others for the bad news		
Talks about the glorious past of the company		
Underestimates the risk ahead		

De-briefing

Have you ever seen the leaders of your organisation do any of the following in a crisis situation?

If you answered:

- *'Yes' to more than 8 statements*: point well taken. Such 'leaders' do exist and in many cases they just destroy their organisations.

- *'Yes' to 3 to 7 statements*: well, nobody is perfect but let's hope that the leaders you have in mind will have the courage to face their weaknesses and show their worth at least from time to time.

- *'Yes' to 1 or 2 statements*: lucky you. Your leaders are very special. They are ready and hopefully will do the right thing to make sure that everything is going to be fine in your organisation!

Now let's see now what people really expect from their leaders in a turbulent time...

The glory of true leadership

"True leadership must be for the benefit of the followers, not the enrichment of the leaders"

- R. Townsend

People who are facing a difficult time expect:

1. To be reassured
2. To trust their leaders
3. To learn how to turn crisis into opportunity

Reassurance

Petrified and panic-stricken people are not only ineffective but they also pose a threat to other people. They block. They resist. They hinder the required changes and eventually contribute to the creation of an ineffective team, organisation, and society. In their despair, they can be very aggressive toward other people. In short, they are dangerous and they don't realise it in most cases.

Therefore, the role of a turnaround leader is:

- To show that they believe in getting out of confusion (even if deep down they also have some major concerns), and to be able to explain some of the critical challenges that the organisation is facing (which is not easy when they do not fully understand the situation themselves).

- To outline the actions that must be taken so that the negative impact of the crisis will be at least minimised if not totally avoided.

- To express themselves not so much through words but more importantly through their behaviour, to show self-confidence and trust in people.

Leadership Tip: The more critical the situation, the more team members expect strong signals from leaders.

Guidance

There is no doubt that most people care not only about their own survival but also about contributing in a professional way to the wellbeing of the company. So, leaders must be very clear about what people can do to help. Many corporations in the past (Digital, Compaq for example) disappeared from the business scene because their top leaders failed to focus on the following priorities:

- To be very open about the seriousness of the situation. It does not help to underrate the risk and create a fake sense of security. People know when something is not right. They expect honest statements as well as coherence between the leaders' words and actions.

- To be diplomatic and empathetic when presenting tough subjects such as layoffs. People by and large will accept layoff decisions as long as they are managed and presented in a fair way.

- To be clear about the business priorities and highlight in a no-nonsense way what everybody can do to participate in the reinvention of the organisation.

Leadership Tip: It is all about TRUST!

From Crisis to Opportunity

It is in a situation like this one (a crisis) that we recognise the true leaders of the world. They do not complain. They do not blame others. They do not hide behind the success of the past. They face the difficulties with:

- Imagination - they have flair and intuition for what will make the team, the company or the society a winner tomorrow. They have ideas about what could happen next. Not esoteric dreams, but insights about the possibilities and the opportunities.

- Courage - they stand up and become living examples of what has to be done. They do not procrastinate and wait for consultants to tell them what their next move must be. Their attitudes and deeds speak much louder than their words.

- Work - there is no escape here. A real crisis requires total involvement. However, leaders must be careful to invest their time, energy and brain power only in what will make a difference.

Leadership Tip: Now is the time when the leaders must stand up and do their job fast and well.

The challenge for leaders now is to assess themselves objectively and to decide where their strengths and weaknesses are in relation to the demanding time.

Below is a simple self-assessment exercise that can provide some food for thought for leaders.

Leadership learning questionnaire 2

Using a scale from 0 to 10, where 0 is not good at all and 10 is very good indeed, answer this question:

As a leader, how good am I at:	Score
Working under pressure	
Being forceful without bringing other people down	
Making fast and to the point decisions	
Keeping the word	
Acting as a role-model	
Enjoying new challenges	
Saying things (that have to be said) without upsetting people	
Improvising if necessary	
Behaving in a credible and reliable way	
Promoting creativity and innovation in your environment	
Setting up priorities	
Getting people energised around carefully selected issues	
Keeping track of what works and what doesn't	
Showing people that I know where I am going	
Taking initiatives	
Feeling good despite what other people say	
Picking up great ideas from others	
Using charm if necessary	
Transferring ideas into actions and results very quickly	
Having doubts and keeping them to myself	
Total score	

<u>De-briefing</u>

If you scored a total of:

- *Between 0 and 75:* It seems that you are lost! Are you there? I strongly suggest that:

    1. You go back to all the items for which you assessed yourself poorly.
    2. Challenge them. Do not take anything for granted.
    3. Give a blank copy of the exercise to somebody who knows you and whom you trust. Ask this person to go through the questionnaire with you, giving you feedback and perhaps validation.

- *Between 76 and 150:* It seems that you are doing well as a crisis leader. It might be a good idea to check on your leadership strengths and validate them by coming up with some concrete and relevant illustrations of what you have done in the past. Make sure that in your team you have people who have the drivers that you do not possess.

- *Between 150 and 200:* Are you serious? It cannot be so good. Actually a score above 150 is maybe a sign of a strong ego or of a natural orientation geared at controlling events and people. Are you really enjoying messy situations? So…be serious now and do the exercise again!

Conclusion

We must face it: in this kind of fast changing world there is no proper conclusion. It is up to the leaders to invent the proper answers to their respective challenges. Consultants and academics do not have the answers (assuming they have the questions). Far from it! But maybe – just maybe – a person next to you has a brilliant idea which will help your organisation to move on and be successful again. After all, leaders are not the only ones with brains.

Leaders as fighters!

Fighters?

Today (even more than in the past) leaders are indeed asked to become champions around some key innovative ideas and invest time and energy in inventing what's not around yet and could be better than what we already have in our organisations and societies.

Yes, leaders must be fighters!

They must fight around three major priorities:

Priority one: Fight for what they believe in.

Priority two: Fight to avoid the tyranny of the average.

Priority three: Fight for the people who work with them.

1. Fight for their dreams

Since the future is uncertain and not predictable in many ways, leaders have no choice but to make the difference and outperform others by inventing tomorrow today. They must see what other do not see (e.g. Steve Jobs) and fight to make it happen. They must dream about a better situation and sell their insights to the people who will help them make them true. They fight and compete even against themselves!

Building on what Anita Roddick (former CEO of Body Shop) said about a corporate vision, we would claim that leaders must set up "dreams with clear-cut deadlines" and then be real shakers and movers!

2. Fight for excellence

A major issue in teams and organisations is that they regularly (and hopelessly) fall into the trap of what we call 'the tyranny of the average'. We have strong evidence that as soon as people get together in the same space and at the same time, they do not go automatically for high quality performance but for average decisions. Voting is going average. Decision making by compromises and consensus is going average. Leaders must be aware of this trap and make sure that at least from time to time they boost up their teams and organisations by allowing some out of the norm behaviour such as being provocative, disagreeing openly with each other, challenging well-established assumptions, being unsatisfied with the quality of a discussion, and sometimes even putting some unrealistic time pressure on people!

3. Fight for people

Maybe the most critical fight for leaders today is to stand up for their people and make sure that they have everything they need to run fast, perform well and enjoy what they do.

They must create a positive environment for performance and …joy. Jim Adamson, the former CEO at NCR (the producer of ATM machines based in Scotland), used to say that 80% of his time was devoted to "taking the road blocks away so that the people can run fast".

There is no question that in a highly empowered world in which people demand a lot from their leaders, the ability to show that one believes in what people think and do is critical. There is nothing more depressing for people at work to see that their leaders are totally uninterested in their ideas and much more interested in the power game than in helping people succeed.

It is quite a sad fact that so many people talk about bottom-up loyalty and that almost nobody mentions top-down loyalty!

Are you a fighting leader?

Just look very quickly at the 10 questions hereunder and answer by yes or no:

	Yes	No
Do you have a tendency to believe that you can do better in your job?		
As a leader, do you trust your intuition?		
Are you good at projecting yourself into the future?		
Do you agree with the 'tyranny of the average' concept?		
Is it alright to challenge you with provocative ideas?		

Do you trust people who are better than you are?		
Is your people's success your success?		
Are you used to fighting on behalf of your people?		
Do you benchmark your organisation's performance against better organisations?		
Are people fighting to work with you?		

De-briefing

- *If you have answered 'yes' to 7 - 10 questions*: you belong to the generation of leaders who are not afraid of taking risk with new ideas, working with great people and searching for the best decisions and actions.

- *If you have answered 'yes' to 4 - 6 questions*: you are fine but maybe a bit too shy in some areas. May we suggest that you go back to your 'no' answers and examine what you could do to be a better leader?

- *If you have answered 'yes' to 1 - 3 questions*: you should maybe ask yourself if leadership is really right for you!

Fighting has always been a must for leaders. The intensity of the fight has not changed over the generations and even centuries - what has changed is the nature of it. The world today requires a different kind of fight and many people are not quite ready for it. Are you? If yes, what are the priorities that you are fighting for in your organisations?

Male or female leadership:
Who is the 'winner'?

(Co-written with Professor Sharon Turnbull, Director of the Research Centre for Applied Leadership at The Leadership Trust)

The questions very few dare to ask (at least openly and candidly) despite (or maybe just because of) their importance.

There is a big debate today around the three following issues:

1.   Are there major differences between male and female leaders' attitudes and behaviours?
2.   How can we explain the fact that in so many organisations there are so few female leaders at the top?
3.   Are male leaders more effective than their female counterparts?

In this short but provocative paper we intend to address the third question. Professor Pierre Casse will argue that male leaders are better equipped to act in the business world whereas Professor Sharon Turnbull will claim that female leaders are at least as equally equipped to play the leadership role if not better. Of course, it is up to the reader to decide on the relevance of the arguments and to make up their minds on what they can get out of the confrontations of ideas and opinions.

Readers should keep in mind that there is no truth other than what they believe to be so. In other words the reader must decide who is the winner in the 'leadership game' and that one way or another both men and woman alike, play a part. In saying so, we assume that there is a winner and we also assume that winning is the name of the 'social game'!

Pierre's Case

Male leadership is the cultural norm

There can be no question that organisations, in both the public and private sectors, have been mainly created by men, for men. Male leaders are therefore better equipped than female leaders to play the leadership role in most corporations. There are at least seven reasons for why this is so. Let's consider each of them in turn as follows:

89

1. *Men are brought up by their parents to play the leadership role*

   In most societies educational systems are such that they prepare little boys to activate in themselves some of the key assumptions and values necessary to play a leadership role later on in their lives. They learn quite early in their childhood to be outspoken, act aggressively and enjoy being in charge.

2. *The distribution of roles in most societies supports men rather than women in the search for, and acceptance of, leadership responsibilities*

   Collective lives in most cultures have been designed, (historically speaking), by men supported by the power system to assume the role of chief of the tribe, king or bishop. The distribution of social roles, (educators, politicians, doctors...), has always been decided by men with a very strong bias towards serving men's interests.

3. *Men have inherited some basic skills that allow them to survive and thrive in tough business environments*

   It seems that men have as parts of their biological make up the qualities required to take risks, decide and impose their decision on other people, including other men. Biologically speaking and at this time in our evolution, it looks like men are better equipped to meet the challenges of the environment: be forceful, push, control, command, etc.

4. *Men want to play the leadership role*

   Men through the ages have developed a taste for leadership that still influences them today. Role models are encouraging them to take charge, to be heroes and to control other people's lives. Therefore, for historical reasons, most men, in most societies expect to be the leaders.

5. *Most men enjoy the power game inherent to leadership*

   This is the key to leadership: power - with all its implications, including the need to influence and control things, situations and people. Men, by and large, love power. They fight for it. They live for it. They die for it.

6. *Male leaders are able to ignore, or control, emotions, something which can inhibit people from being effective leaders*

One of the most important leadership requirements is to be able to manage one's own emotions. Male leaders acknowledge the importance of emotions and are able to play on them without getting too dependent on this dimension of life. They like to appear cool, rational and in control.

7. *Men are not going to give up the privileges and advantages connected with executive roles*

Men are so used to having the leadership role in most environments that they are not going to pass it on to women with ease. They will fight to keep it. They will use all the reasons and arguments in the book to conserve it. They will concede to women the leadership parts they see as not that critical or very important. Moreover it seems that the trend is for men to give away those leadership roles connected to the past and invent new and glorifying ones for the future.

Male leadership is toxic and inadequate

And yet one must admit that if male leadership is the cultural norm in today's business world, it is also true that our current situation is not necessarily good for the future of our collective life. There are at least three major reasons why a better distribution of leadership power between men and women could help us be better off in the future:

1. *Men are leading in toxic way*

It does not take long when working in a corporation to realise that many working environments (teams, business units, organisations), are toxic and unhealthy. The dominant male leadership style very often gives rise to aggression, unethical behaviours, wild competition, lack of consideration and moderation. In short, male leadership leads to a toxic environment in which people experience fear and the loss of their dignity. Testosterone does not help people to work healthily together.

2. *We need more women at the top of most organisations*

Yes, people would have a lot to gain if more women were to be found in key leadership positions in the corporate world. The issue is that these days in many cases women who go to the top and acquire as much power as the men do lose their feminine values in the process. They adjust themselves to the male value system to get the expected, and in most cases well deserved, promotions. That's not what organisations need to re-invent themselves. They are desperate to get women in executive roles with their particular way to look at the world and re-orient how people get together to invent, produce and sell goods and services.

3.   *The new world requires new leadership mindsets*

The new communication technologies are impacting the definition of roles and the distribution of power in a dramatic way. It seems that the yesterday way of looking at men and women in business and politics is being re-visited and changed fundamentally and irreversibly. It is by inventing a new world (global, concerned with sustainable development and ethical behaviours…) and by using the new technologies that women will probably go into the new power game with a strong competitive advantage!

<u>Sharon's Case</u>

Women's leadership is more subtle but women leaders are a force to be reckoned with

I do not believe that men are born to lead and that women are born to nurture. There are many matriarchal societies where the women are the clear leaders, despite the biological demands on them to give birth and care for their offspring. Even in societies where men purport to hold the key leadership positions in society, politics, or business, we often find that it is the women behind the scenes who are quietly leading the male leaders. Quiet leadership has for women been the name of the game for centuries, as women have found many ways to influence without threatening those with formal power. The idea that men are biologically more suited to leadership has been perpetuated by men over many generations in order to hold onto the power that this affords them. This is clearly a myth that has suited many men, and enabled them to maintain the status quo in society! The continuity of this stereotype despite many years of equal opportunity legislation and despite the emancipation of women in so many other ways has been in their interest. Why allow the other 52% of the population to compete for power?

Female leadership is the way of the future

So what are the qualities of leadership that women have learned as a result of so many years of finding ways to circumvent the constraints of a patriarchal system?

1. *Having been overlooked for leadership positions for so long as a result of the 'gentlemen's club', women have long found alternative ways to lead in organisations*

    They often lead in a much smarter and more subtle way, by building long-standing relationships and networks. As a result of years of discrimination by men, and the reinforcement of a very tough glass-ceiling, many women have learned extraordinary networking skills. Support from other women, but also from sympathetic men in organisations, are essential to women leaders and this has enhanced their ability to establish vital relationships.

2. *Women are frequently more intuitive than men*

    Their leadership is therefore often highly people-focused. The ability of women leaders to consider the needs of followers as individuals gives them a great advantage when winning their support and loyalty, and well as their commitment to organisational goals. Women leaders are sensitive to the needs of those at the bottom of the hierarchy, because they have usually started there themselves and had to struggle for recognition. They understand powerlessness, and therefore often delight in empowering others.

3. *Women often play a longer game, seeing beyond the immediate into the future*

    Women know how to wait and be patient. Men are more likely to focus on immediate results. This means that women leaders are often more strategic and more able to see the bigger picture, an important asset in today's fast changing world.

4. *Women are less blindly individualistic and competitive than many men, and more able to collaborate, and build creative connections with others, even with their competitors*

    Women know that the success of the team is also their success. Teamwork and sharing are a natural part of their leadership repertoire.

They are comfortable with the idea of shared or dispersed leadership.

5. *Women leaders tend to be much less ego-centric than many male leaders*

They have learned to submerge their egos so that the men around them do not see them as a threat. In so doing they learn ways to impress others without boasting or succumbing to narcissism. They expect to be recognised for achievement, and not rhetoric, and are frustrated when their male counterparts are duped by egocentric talk instead of results! Those women who do adopt male competitive and individualistic behaviours are often not liked by other women leaders, as their behaviour is seen as too combative and even aggressive. By contrast men who learn to lead collaboratively are increasingly being seen as more prepared for today's complex world.

6. *Emotional intelligence is a construct that captures the essence of many women leaders*

It is at the heart of how we lead, and only in recent years has it been discovered by men to have a value. Interestingly, this secret weapon of women leaders was exposed by Daniel Goleman, a man who thought he was onto something entirely new!

At last, women have started to break though the glass ceiling and into the boardroom. This has created a new dynamic, and many men have acknowledged the value of their female colleagues in bringing different perspectives to problem solving and strategy development. The human aspects of a decision, for example, are no longer the last to be considered. Women have brought a powerful balance of rational analysis and intuition, as well as collaboration and holistic thinking.

However, a new phenomenon has recently been identified by Michelle Ryan and colleagues from Exeter University. They have noted that women who do break through the glass ceiling are more likely to subsequently encounter a glass cliff than their male counterparts. What is the glass cliff? It represents a precarious leadership situation from which a leader is likely to fail and fall. This research has shown that women often find themselves in risky leadership roles, those with a high likelihood of failure, and no safety net. Many women leaders lose their hard-earned places in the boardroom as a result. But are they deliberately placed in these roles by malicious male colleagues, or do they choose these roles for themselves? Researchers are now focusing on finding the answers to these important questions that will undoubtedly affect the future of women in the boardroom.

Lack of self-confidence as a result of years of stereotyping, exacerbated by time out of the workplace by many mothers, has for many years held back highly capable women. Women dislike boasting and will tend to downplay their achievements in comparison with men who tend to exaggerate theirs! The glass ceiling and glass cliff are not helping women leaders to build their self-confidence, and they enable men to continue the myth that they are more capable leaders than women. Women leaders no longer need to feel that they have to act like men. We can instead lead effectively by recognising our own unique capabilities, and those many skills that we have developed over generations when leading from behind, or below, or from positions of apparent powerlessness. Women have always known that position in the hierarchy has little to do with leadership. Women leaders are a force to be reckoned with!

Egocentric or humble? Leadership in question

(Co-written with Professor Sharon Turnbull, Director of the Research Centre for Applied Leadership at The Leadership Trust)

"A leader is a dealer in hope"

- Napoleon Bonaparte

Introduction

Who is right! Who is wrong?

"There are two sides to every issue: one side is right and the other is wrong, but the middle way is always evil".

- Ayn Rand

Many people, including scholars and practitioners in the leadership field, have been debating what makes a good leader since the beginning of time. It is not an easy question and let's face it, the conventional answer - it depends - is far from satisfactory. It is too simple, too easy, too wrong.

This paper will see two people committed to advancing the debate are trying to provide a direct answer to the question at hand. However, they disagree on the following key issue: the 'stamina' and 'self-centred drive' of the leader as key success factors in leadership.

One position, put forward by Professor Casse, claims that effective leaders need to be egocentric (i.e. self-confident), self-centred and ready and willing to bask in glory following every success. In other words, they should look for recognition when it is well deserved and use it to mobilise other people. The claim is that winners are magnet leaders. Historically, he suggests, all leaders who have had an impact on the world were strongly egocentric.

The other position, put forward by Professor Turnbull, is based on the belief that a good leader should be able to succeed but remain humble. Her idea is that humility is a key characteristic of good leadership. It leads to respect and loyalty. Winners do not need to show off and impress people with their glory. Their humility speaks for itself. It reassures and impresses people who then give them their trust and commitment.

Both authors are requesting readers to consider each position and decide for themselves which one they believe is right. The readers' decision should be based on their own experience and knowledge of the field but avoiding the easy way out by answering, 'It depends!'

The egocentric view - Professor Pierre Casse

"He that humbleth himself wishes to be exalted"

- Friedrich Nietzsche

"Don't be so humble - you're not that great"

- Golda Meir

There are at least five reasons why being egocentric is a necessity in leadership:

1. To love one's self is critical for impacting others. As someone once said, "All living things are alive because of selfishness". How can you lead others if you do not first believe in yourself? Self-confidence is a key to leadership success. Doubt and hesitation are not good characteristics in leadership. Effective leaders must project an image of certitude and conviction. This is only possible if they have a high opinion of themselves. The ability to lead one's self is a prerequisite in leadership.

2. Leadership without power is useless. As the philosopher Spinoza put it, "The power of individual choice is stronger than any collective seeking to repress it". Being brilliant without the power necessary to implement great ideas is useless. Leaders must therefore value power. They must know how to acquire it, use it properly and expand it. They must also convey a message to other people (i.e. power is good and enjoyable). It is also very important for them to demonstrate that they can share the power with people who are loyal, dedicated and performing well. It is clear that people who have to work with powerless people have a tendency to disrespect them.

3. Self-energising is a pre-condition for leadership success. According to Edison, "The first requisite for success is the ability to apply our physical and mental energies to one problem incessantly, without growing

weary". Vitality is critical in leadership. If leading is about changing things around, then the ability to energise one's self as well as others is vital. Energy goes with ego. Highly energised people are perceived as self-centred. People accept it because they do feel deep down that those with energy and stamina will get them wherever they wish to be. A high energy level is very attractive.

4. To be proud of one's own actions is a leadership must. "No one has a greater asset for his business than a man's pride in his work" (H. Ballou). Pride is a virtue. It is what is needed to outperform one's self as well as other people. Great leaders are, generally speaking, proud of their actions and their successes. Pride is "what separates excellence from mediocrity" (W. Blake). Successful leaders are not afraid of showing off when they have been successful because it reassures people and gives them confidence. They like to work with leaders who are committed and proud of their achievements.

5. Great leaders are not afraid of visibility. As Oscar Wilde observed, "It is only shallow people who do not judge by appearances". Special leaders are looking for visibility. They like to be acknowledged and recognised. Their motivation comes from their conviction that other people believe in them and that they expect high quality outcomes from their actions. They know that to be known is a key leadership success factor. Visibility is a pre-condition for leading others: how could people follow leaders if they do not know who they are?

The case for humility – Professor Sharon Turnbull

"Humility is the only true wisdom by which we prepare our minds for all the possible changes of life"

- George Arliss

"Humility is the solid foundation of all virtues"

- Confucius

"It is unwise to be too sure of one's own wisdom. It is healthy to be reminded that the strongest might weaken and the wisest might err"

- Gandhi

Pierre Casse's argument for egocentric leaders is persuasive but dangerous! There is an extraordinary amount of research to show the dangers of narcissism both for leaders themselves and for their followers. For leaders, egocentrism frequently leads in the end to humiliating derailment. For followers, their experience is of alienation from these self-centred and unsympathetic individuals with little if any emotional intelligence.

Ego and unbridled desire for power is responsible for many ruined organisations and countries, destroyed by pathologically flawed, ego-centric leaders. History is full of their tragic legacies. Idi Amin, Adolf Hitler, Sadam Hussein, Slobodan Milosevic, and Robert Mugabe, for example, show how destructive narcissism and the ego drive can be. Even in the less malevolent case of Tony Blair, we see how his meteoric success was swiftly followed by his downfall, but not before Britain found itself embroiled in a futile and harmful war. This has been diagnosed by many as an extreme case of hubris. Lord Owen, for example, in his book, *In Sickness and in Power: Illness in Heads of Government During the Last 100 Years* argues that, after 1999 at the outset of the Kosovo conflict, and later with Iraq, Blair gradually tipped into "excessive self-confidence, restlessness and inattention to detail." [1]

In business, there are many similar stories, one of the most recent and well known being the story of Fred 'the Shred' Goodwin, RBS's Chief Executive, who not only brought down his own bank, but also contributed in large measure to the banking crisis as a whole. This story typifies the destructive outcome of self love and greed, two fundamental drivers of ego-centric leadership. Sarah Arnott of the Independent wrote at the time of his downfall:

"How the mighty are falling. The rise and fall of Sir Fred Goodwin is the classic tale of vaulting ambition which o'erleaps itself, of hubris brought low by the very qualities which led to such stellar success". [2]

Why are such leaders so dangerous and why do they eventually derail?

1. They stop listening to others.

2. They start to believe unquestionably that they are right and that everybody who opposes them is wrong.

3. They believe themselves to be infallible.

4. Their purpose becomes their own self aggrandisement above all else.

5. Followers eventually turn against them.

"In all great deceivers a remarkable process is at work to which they owe their power. In the very act of deception with all its preparations, the dreadful voice, expression, and gestures, they are overcome by their belief in themselves; it is this belief which then speaks, so persuasively, so miracle-like, to the audience."

- Friedrich Nietzsche, *'The Genealogy of Morals'*

When MBA students are asked who they believe to be good leaders, their answers invariably include in their top ten Nelson Mandela, Mahatma Gandhi, and Mother Teresa. What these leaders have in common that makes them great is humility.

So why do great leaders need humility?

1. Humility enables a leader to recognise and unlock the value and potential of those around them, and make use of all of their talents. To listen to others is one of the most important elements of leadership. Ego-centric leaders don't do this. Their own opinion is the only one that really counts. They only pay lip service to the opinions of others. Humility is a trait that is much loved by followers. It motivates, energises, and builds self- esteem in followers by its explicit recognition of their value.

2. Humility does not mean weak. It requires strength and self-awareness to develop humility. It is easy to be driven by ego! Leaders who have learned humility are seen by their followers as strong, purposeful and reflective. These great and rare leaders have often struggled for many years to follow this humble path. If we reflect on the world's great religious leaders - Jesus, the Prophet Mohammed, and the Buddha, for example - all are known for their enormous humility, and all exemplify for their followers characteristics that are virtuous and 'ideal' in a leadership role model.

3. Humility enables a leader to direct his or her attention on a purpose and outside themselves. Jim Collins, in his book *Good to Great*, shows how 'level 5' leaders focus not on their own needs and wants, but on the purpose of building their businesses to become great. In an interview with Fortune magazine, Collins confirms the vital role of humility in leadership success:

"The best CEOs in our research display tremendous ambition for their company combined with the stoic will to do whatever it takes, no matter

how brutal (within the bounds of the company's core values), to make the
company great. Yet at the same time they display a remarkable humility
about themselves, ascribing much of their own success to luck, discipline
and preparation rather than personal genius". [3]

4. Humility enables leadership to become a shared process and
   acknowledges that decision-making is rarely effective when it remains
   in the hands of a single individual, particularly one who believes him/
   herself to be right all the time! In the UK, for example, there has recently
   been much criticism of the inability of successive prime ministers to
   share leadership with their Cabinet Ministers. The many flawed decisions
   of recent times are the result.

5. Leaders with humility are more likely to follow an ethical path than
   those driven primarily by the need for personal success. They value the
   importance of society, and of the world, and are guided by a desire for
   the good of many, rather than simply the good of themselves. In today's
   troubled world where we are indisputably facing a crisis of ethics that
   is leading to today's global problems - climate change, poverty, food
   shortage, political unrest and terrorism - these are a legacy that we risk
   leaving for future generations. The world does not need more ego driven
   leaders. We are critically in need of leaders who can see the big global
   picture, and then act for the benefit of humanity and future generations,
   as well as for their colleagues and their organisations.

The arguments that have been made above in favour of humility as the most
important leadership virtue of a good leader speak for themselves. In the wise
words of Benjamin Franklin: "A man wrapped up in himself makes a very
small bundle".

In conclusion (tentatively)

The two writers do not want to conclude with a compromise and state that
the activation of both human traits (selfishness and humility) can be effective
or not according to the situations and the circumstances the leaders are
facing. That would be both too easy and misleading.

This is not the purpose of the article.

Not at all! They want readers to think about themselves and decide on their
own if their natural orientations and drives are effective i.e. in line with
the requirements of their environments and the expectations of the people

around?

More important, is the way they are (as leaders and human beings) the way they want to be?

References

[1] Owen, D. (2008). *In Sickness and in Power: Illness in Heads of Government During the Last 100 Years.* London: Methuen.

[2] Arnott, S. (2008, October 14). 'The Rise and Fall of "Fred the Shred"'. *The Independent.* Retrieved April 15, 2009, from: http://www.independent.co.uk/news/business/analysis-and-features/the-rise-and-fall-of-fred-the-shred-960336.html

[3] Boyle, M., & Collins, J. (2007, March 14). 'Q&A with Management Guru Jim Collins'. *Fortune.* Retrieved April 15, 2009, from:http://money.cnn.com/magazines/fortune/fortune_archive/2007/02/19/8400260/index.htm

Leadership and the power of expectations

(Co-written with Renn Zaphiropoulos, former CEO of Varsatec & Corporate Vice-President of the Xerox Corporation)

"Success is about exceeding expectations in such a way that the actual outcome of an action exceeds the expressed expectation by at least 1. Success= Actual:Expected>1. This is the equation of winning"

- Renn Zaphiropoulos

"So many people have been so conditioned by their leaders' expectations that they have forgotten to live their own lives altogether.

- Pierre Casse

Who needs expectations?

"The first task of a leader is to keep hope alive"

- Joe Batten

This article is written in cooperation with a very successful (and very wise) business leader: Renn Zaphiropoulos[1]. We wish to discuss the issues of leadership and expectations, which is particularly pertinent in light of this issue's theme of global challenges, from both the point of view of the practitioner and the academic.

First, some initial comments from the business leader's perspective:

Man is a measuring human being. Mankind is full of measurements and evaluations about everything we do, like and dislike. To measure anything one has to adopt a standard and this is where expectations come from. An expectation is a cautious forecast of things turning out good or bad according to the information we have at the present. We have expectations about everything even if we don't articulate them. As a matter of fact, our culture is one which discourages people to say what they expect of each other. You have to be nice and not demanding and go with the flow if you are a compassionate person. These are not the characteristics of a leader.

A leader acts properly when he or she makes their expectations clear of themselves and of other people. If I enter into a relationship I do it on the basis that it will be pleasant and rewarding and mutually satisfying. It is possible that what I expected does not occur and on this basis I am critical of a relationship and possibly I would end it. If on the contrary, the relationship turns out to be better than I expected I hope it will be long lasting and mutually beneficial. Expectations can vary in numbers, attitudes, feelings, etc. Very civilized people do not say what they expect of each other. They hesitate in being blunt and real. So, they act in a disapproving way but they do not announce the cause of the disparity. Leaders can express their expectations without threatening, without being abusive, or authoritative.

Next, the academic perspective:

The main theme is based on the following assumption: leaders with high hopes or very positive expectations (self and others) are much more effective than those with low hope. In other words optimistic leaders are by and large much more successful than pessimistic ones.

What we mean by expectations (as a working definition for the sake of this paper), is the projection that somebody is making about oneself or others regarding one's own ability (or other people's for that matter) to:

- Think, feel and behave in a certain way
- Implement some actions and achieve a set of objectives
- Change and grow.

There is no question that expectations are important in all human lives. They create the tension between what is and what could be that we need as individuals, groups, organisations and even countries to move forward and develop ourselves. Without expectations, life is flat and in many cases boring.

So nature gave us the ability to stretch ourselves through the production of ideas about 'what could be better'.

Some people go as far as claiming that expectations are the necessary dreams that ultimately project all human beings into the art of 're-inventing ourselves and becoming'! They perceive them as a critical ingredient of individual growth and development and social/economic progress.

To summarise, the ability to produce expectations is necessary for three reasons:

1. They allow us to project ourselves into the future, dream about what could be and fight for it.
2. Through the production of expectations, we at least have the feeling that there is hope and that we could do better.

3. Without expectations status quo would be the rule and…quite depressing for many people.

But…

Some major issues about expectations have been very well identified too and they are:

1. They can be so ambitious that they are totally unrealistic and even in some cases destructive.
2. Some people have been very good at imposing their expectations on other people who unconsciously, in many cases, do not even realise that they are manipulated.
3. Some expectations are not quite right or ethically correct.

Managing expectations: the challenge

> *"People will exceed targets they set themselves"*
>
> - Gordon Dryden

Idea 1: Success is about exceeding expectations

The academic view:

It seems indeed that to be successful one needs to have ambitious goals and expectations. One still needs to define success! Is it money, prestige, status, quality of personal life, social contributions…? There are so many definitions of success. It all depends on the individuals' needs and wants. Having stated that, it is also clear that 'exceeding expectations' can have a few drawbacks:

*   One can get used to exceeding our expectations and get into a spiral of pressure and stress. One gets disappointed when the expectations are not overwhelming met.
*   One then learns how to go low with expectations so that it is not too difficult to exceed them.
*   Most people learn quickly to keep an eye on what managers expect and

to align the personal expectations to those of the boss.
- There is also the non-negligible peer pressure that can lead to some escalation and the creation of a sick environment.
- Exceeding our expectations can be a source of over-confidence for some individuals.

Another issue is the fact (as stated by Adam Smith) that a greater part of men have an "overwhelming conceit of their abilities". This can destroy them…

The business view:

In business we always have to give out forecasts to our managers so they can expect the right behaviour and results. Since success is measured by an overachievement with respect to expectations, many people will downplay their forecast so over-achievement is guaranteed - this is called 'sandbagging'.

When you are a manager you have to motivate your people to be the best they can be. This is why the expectations in this case strain the capability of a person so that they can do the impossible. Care must be taken so that what you expect of people is not that much more than they can do, because this will not motivate them, it will break them down. Many children complain that their parents are expecting them to do the impossible. Setting up expectations is an art form. It is the kind of thing that on the one hand it strains and makes the person anxious, on the other hand it is a motivating force to be better than you think you are. This sometimes works wonders.

Idea 2: Managing expectations is a leadership must

The academic view:

Managing expectations can be seen by many people as a pure manipulation of some human beings by others who seem to have more power and therefore the ability to impose their views on what's good and not so good for other people. So the expression 'managing expectations' has in many contexts (including the corporate one) a negative connotation.

Leaders therefore must be careful and make sure that the expectations are:

- Mainly the expression of the individual's aspirations.
- Encouraged as much as possible as long as they seem realistic and yet a source of positive tension for the people, the team and the organisation.
- Discouraged—if destructive and totally out of order—with sensitivity and diplomacy.

The business view:

In developing real expectations one has to grow up and see things in an updated manner so they are on the right track and at the same time they should understand that all opposites co-exist. So if we want success, we must expect a certain amount of failure happening at the same time. This helps us take things less seriously without de-motivating us towards a lesser performance. If I fail and I am grown up, I don't blow my brains out, I think there is work to be done and I am spurned to fix my problem. The fact is I discovered that quality, happiness and success have the same definition. They occur when the actual (really what happens) as compared to the expected is larger than one. This indicates that our happiness, quality and success are our own doing. It is not measured by itself, but it is always against a standard which we have set for ourselves and other people. Sometimes the performance is perfect but the expectation was wrong. I have missed many forecasts on the basis of wrong expectations while the actual performance was acceptable.

Idea 3: The 'Pygmalion effect' is still critical in leadership

The academic view:

Professor Rosenthal from Columbia University was right when his research showed that the expectations of managers regarding the team members' ability to perform have a tremendous impact on the real performance of the same people. In other words if employees believe that their managers think that they can perform at a certain level, they will adjust their performance to the perceived level: high or low! So the projections of the leaders' expectations onto other people can play magic!

The business view:

Leadership has to include the ability to convince people when you make your expectations clear. You make people feel that they can accomplish what is requested by the reasons you explain to them. This is where an authoritative attitude falls short. The subject will say "what do expect us to be? Not ourselves?" Brutal dictators do not justify what they expect, you are supposed to obey because they are the authority. This does not work in a place where you want people to be creative, inventive and brilliant. People who over-achieve their expectations beyond their dreams, lose humility and think themselves competent instead of lucky. To really be a success you have to be wrong on the right side. I am sure that Bill Gates didn't expect to be the richest man in the world, but things turned out that way. He was competent in exploited unforeseen benevolent circumstances.

Tentative conclusions

Reflecting on expectations, one can keep in mind that:

- Despite the power of dreams, there are still a lot of individuals who prefer to enjoy what they have today rather than investing in some hypothetical better future (Adam Smith).
- Many men and women still strongly believe that they do not exist to meet others' expectations (F. Perls).
- Expectations are basically desires which are in so many cases a source of pain and suffering (Schopenhauer).

Questions for the readers (an expectation scorecard)

Please answer the following question by yes or no.

By and large I think I am inclined to:	Yes	No
See the good things of life		
Perceive myself as a winner		
Value more the future than the present		
Fight for my ideas		
Visualise myself in the future		
Have great ambitions about my life		
Imagine what my destiny could be		
Believe that tomorrow will be better than today		
Put the pressure on myself		
Work very hard to make it happen		

De-briefing

- *'Yes' for 7-10:* there is a good chance that you live by your expectations. You are driven by them. Your motivation is maybe coming from your dreams about 'what could be'. Be careful though and make sure that you are ready not to exceed or even meet your expectations. It could hurt you a lot since you have invested so much into building your future.

- *'Yes' for 4-6:* it could mean that you live in both the present and the future time. Hopefully you are able to reconcile the demands of your current situation with your expectations for tomorrow. That requires some good use of the tension that could be created by the needs of today and the demands of your plan for after.

- *'Yes' for 1-3:* you should maybe have a good look at where you stand with your life. You are either fully satisfied with what you have (or who you are) or you are maybe struggling with the requirements of your present situation that you have no dreams about the future! You are perhaps then in what we call a 'survival mode'. Be aware that people who have no dreams can get depressed quite easily.

A sample of leadership expectations

Below are the results of a short survey conducted amongst both leaders and non-leaders to ascertain the expectations of leaders. What do you think? And where do you stand as a leader among these attributes?

Leaders expect their team members to be:

- Loyal
- Bold and able to take (calculated) risk
- Outspoken
- Passionate
- Honest
- Effective
- Imaginative

Team members expect their leaders to be:

- Supportive

- Clear and informative
- Decisive
- Ready to stand up on behalf of the team members
- Able to provide the proper recognition
- Fair
- Concerned about the creation of a healthy environment

Jumping into a new life - a leadership quiz

"Life is too short to be miserable"

- Anonymous

"Life is too short to be small."

- Benjamin Disraeli

Taking Stock

You have just finished school or attended a training seminar and you are wondering: "what's next"?! Or you have just decided to move on with your life and change direction. Or, still, you have lost your job and wonder how you are going to survive.

Your next move could be quite an important (even critical) one and therefore better to think twice about:

- Your strengths: What is it that you do well and enjoy? There is a point in anybody's life when it is much more effective to build on the strengths instead of struggling with the weaknesses. Deep down inside, 'one is what one is'.

- Your priorities in life: Better to know what you want to achieve with your life. In other words, do you have a clear idea of what you want to achieve and accomplish with that precious gift that is 'being alive'? If not, it could be a good idea to take stock of where you are and what you want to be in three or five years from now.

- Your constraints: Let's also be realistic. Life can be difficult and loaded with obstacles and problems. There are times when it can be harsh and painful. The struggle for life is not a vain expression. We do fight and sometimes lose…Facing reality (including when it is painful) is a life must.

A key to success: know what you want!

To be aware of our deep aspirations can be a premise for good decisions in your life. What is it that you want to get (now or as soon as possible)? Check the list hereunder and decide on what's actually critical for you. Pick up the three most important ones:

- Money
- Fame
- Love
- Power
- Learning
- Family
- Health
- Sex
- Friendship
- Spirituality

Or…maybe something that does not appear in this list?

Are you (really) ready?

Below is a little quiz that can help you think through with your decision. Answer the following questions with a simple 'yes' or 'no':

Do You:	Yes	No
Feel that you have reached a point when you must change		
Know now what your personal strengths and weaknesses are		
Intend to use most of what you have got from nature, education and social experience		
Feel ready to fight for your survival and success		
Have a clear idea of where you want to be in five years time		
Know how to get there		
Feel ready to move forward and take some risk		
Know that you must move fast		

See yourself as a 'winner'		
Feel energised and optimistic		

De-briefing

- *If you have between 7 and 10 'yes' answers:* Congratulations! You know where you are as well as where you are going. My advice: Just keep going. It seems that you are on the right track.

- *If you have between 4 and 6 'yes' answers:* Well, there is some ambiguity in your position regarding your life. It seems that do have some idea about where you are and where you would like to be but is it not yet quite crystallised in your mind. My advice: Do not hesitate to invest some time in reflecting on your current situation and prepare a simple plan for action. Focus on two or three priorities and then go for it.

- *If you have between 1 and 3 'yes' answers:* It seems that you are maybe lost and wonder what this is all about. You are maybe both sceptical and even a bit cynical about the possibility to lead your own life. You could think that destiny is destiny and there is nothing you can do about it. My advice: think twice. You are right that there is no need to push the river that flows anyway. However, there is much more room for initiative (with a range of given options) than we think.

Social grooming - a new side to leadership?

'You scratch my back and I scratch yours – and we are all fine and happy'

Do we really need each other? If we do, what for?

Social grooming

Social grooming can be defined as the process by which human beings fulfill one of their basic instincts (i.e. to socialise, cooperate and learn from each other.)

The hypothesis in a nutshell:

We strongly believe that the function, or raison d'être, of the corporation must be revisited, reviewed and re-invented at the beginning of this new century. Of course the primary role of an organisation, at least in the private sector, is still to manage the processes by which people invent, produce and sell goods and services. However, we see a trend in the business community today toward paying ever more attention to both its external and internal social responsibility.

The external dimension is growing fast and has been defined as 'being a good citizen', and caring about the quality of life (sustainable development) in our societies. The internal one is still in its infancy. It refers to organisations giving people not only a fair chance to use their talents and perform well but also an opportunity to grow as individuals and become 'better human beings'. It seems that leaders have a new challenge at hand.

Social grooming: a new leadership must?

It seems that social grooming is critical in the creation and maintenance of a healthy and performing organisational environment. Leaders must invest time and energy in making sure that people have a fair chance to:

1. Talk to each other about things that are not necessarily work related: Grooming and Communication.
2. Experience the very important social process of give and take: Grooming and Reciprocity.

3. Learn from each other and grow from the social stimulation or brain interface: Grooming and Mind Expansion.

Grooming and communication

Organisations have become the centre of human interactions and people are in need of meaningful interfaces with other human beings. This is the case more so today than ever before due to the emergence of new communication technologies which tend to isolate people from each other.

The leader must create space and time for people to experience and enjoy social interactions that are not job related because it reinforces peoples' closeness and gives them personal satisfaction. It helps to improve the quality of life.

Grooming and reciprocity

Reciprocity is the name of the social game. Work is increasingly becoming a give and take process. People are basically selfish (nothing wrong with that) and are becoming more and more demanding in terms of self interest.

Grooming will help the team member to cooperate more effectively and benefit from the social synergy. They want to feel that the deal is fair. They expect their leaders to show them that it is not just a job but a real opportunity to fulfill their aspirations and become what they are deep down inside – to be true to themselves.

Grooming and mind expansion

There is no doubt that a human brain which is not exposed to another human brain does not grow. Leaders will have to pay more attention to the need people have to live up to their potential. They must help people discover through the social grooming process that they have talents that they were not aware of.

Grooming guidelines for leaders

What's in it for you as a leader?

Keep in mind that social grooming is also good for the organisation. Leaders may:

1. Make the difference by inventing an environment in which people experience meaningful events, respect the leader and help him, or her, to grow too!
2. Use social grooming as a fuse so that conflicts and confrontations between individuals do not go too far and do not become too destructive. Leaders then have a better life.
3. Become a 'magnet leader' to attract the best performers within the organisation and therefore enhance their career prospects and the performance of the organisation.

In order to check on your Social Grooming Intelligence, take a look at the statements below and assess yourself on a scale of 0 to 10 whereby:

0 = Not good at all
5 = Sometimes good
10 = Very good

As a leader, how good am I at:	Score
Giving people space	
Showing 'what's in it for them'	
Encouraging the organisation of social events	
Giving people time to relax and chat during the working hours	
Inviting people to your house	
Making sure that people bring their hobbies into the work place	
Being informal	

Helping people to exchange non-work related ideas with each other	
Challenging people with out of the box ideas	
Designing an environment so that people can smile and laugh from time to time	
Inviting the spouses to attend some social events at the office	
Accepting pets in the office	
Providing a place where people can go when they are stressed out or tired	
Allowing people to surf the internet to explore new web sites according to their personal interest	
Encouraging people to share vacation time together (i.e. adventure types)	
Accepting that people use their mobile phones at any time during work (even in meetings)	
Surprising people with special guests and events	
Using unconventional ways to work together, e.g. meeting in the middle of the night	
Sharing information on your private life with team members	
Stimulating people's curiosity	
Total score	

De-briefing

- *If your score is between 0 and 50*: There is a strong possibility that you are not interested in any kind of social activities during the working hours. Work is work! For you the time at work should be devoted to producing and delivering. Forget about that nonsense of socialising and feeling good about each other. Be careful because you could be perceived by the people around you (including your boss or bosses) as being insensitive and missing the minimum of social intelligence to succeed in the organisation.

- *If your score is between 50 and 80:* Good for you! Apparently you are able to pay attention to peoples' emotional needs and expectations. You know that happy people perform much better than unhappy ones. But alongside this motivation of yours there is also a strong possibility that you believe that the corporate world has a new role to play in today's world – and you want to be part of that transformation process.

- *If your score is between 80 and 100:* It is maybe time for you to think about switching to a social (non-profit maybe?) organisation and take great pleasure in managing a highly convivial environment. Keep in mind that in the business community people must still perform and… enjoy!

Conclusion

Social grooming is part of human nature. We cannot live alone. We do not grow isolated from others. The people I work with can be opportunities for me to discover myself and expand from the experience.

Grooming Intelligence: is this the new leadership challenge – one beyond Human Resources and Talent Management?

Discussion questions

Questions for the readers:

1. Is social grooming part of your corporate culture? Do you think it is / would be effective?
2. What do your team members they think of, and expect from, social grooming?
3. Is your boss a social grooming leader? If not what can you do to get him or her there?

Leadership & luck:
Are you a lucky leader?

"Is he lucky?"

- Napoleon Bonaparte (before giving a promotion to an officer)

"If one is lucky, a solitary fantasy can totally transform one million realities"

- Maya Angelou

"Luck affects everything; let your hook always be cast; in the stream where you least expect it, there will be a fish"

- Ovid

"To succeed in life you need three things: a bit of intelligence; to work very hard; some luck"

- Voltaire

A very old predicament

The phenomenon of good and bad luck was noted a long time ago, if not at the very beginning of our existence. Can we succeed in life if we are not lucky? In other words, is it enough to be clever and to work very hard to achieve our goals? It often seems that we need a bit of support from the environment, the situation we are in, and from the people we interact with. Moreover, we also need a bit of help from circumstances that are beyond our control and can yet influence our success in a drastic way. Luck must be around at some critical times.

We would like to propose the following working definition of luck: *"Luck can be defined as a factor that can by itself explain why an action has been successful without having any rational predisposition to be such."*

The expression 'they were lucky!' means that the individuals concerned have been successful not (only) because of their good work, intelligence and perseverance but also and maybe essentially because of some unexplainable support that came from the environment, the timing, or the people. Isn't it true that there are times when we do everything right and yet the result is simply not there? We then wonder: why not? What was missing? And the answer can be: no luck or bad luck! (There are also times when we do all the wrong things and get great results!)

We do say about some people that they are lucky, i.e. that they benefit from that 'invisible factor' that supports their endeavor in almost all situations. The outcome of their actions is almost in contradiction with what a rational, logical assessment would have predicted. Sometimes it may look unfair to many people. Why them? Why not me? Or sometimes people will say: "he has been lucky",, meaning "he has succeeded despite his wrong decision and ineffective behaviour."

The lucky questionnaire

Assess your LQ using measures 0, 5, and 10, where 0 = not at all; 5 = from time to time; and 10 = very often:

It often happens that I:	Score
Am surprised by the results of my own actions	
Benefit from unexpected support	
Experience shifts in the environment at the right time	
Get help from people whom I know nothing about	
Do the right thing at the right time without even thinking about it	
Rely on favorable circumstances to achieve great things	
Make mistakes and yet succeed	
Am criticised by others for what they call my easy successes	
Trust that events unfold in my favour	
Think that fate is in my favour	
Total score	

De-briefing:

- *For a score of 70 to 100:* I do not believe it! What are you doing here? You should be sitting at the casino table…

- *For a total score of 30 to 70:* Welcome to the majority of people. You do experience that little push from time to time and yet you must be careful because it is not steady and predictable. Better to bet on your good work and willpower to succeed.

- *For a total score of 0 to 30:* It seems that you are not the kind of person who can rely on luck to achieve and be happy. Your LQ is quite low. Better to work on it…(read on!)

The above observations raise three major leadership questions:

1. Is luck a leadership key success factor?
2. Can one manage luck, i.e. activate it and channel it?
3. What can one do if one does not have any?

Is luck a leadership 'key success factor'?

Can we succeed without a minimum of luck? The answer is obviously yes! However, there is no doubt that brain power plus dedication will be much more effective if the following three factors are supportive of our decisions and actions:

- The timing is right: "I launch a new project without any special thought given to the timing and to my surprise it was the right time."
- The environment is right: "I did what I had to do and got some totally unexpected support from the environment that I would have thought hostile to my ideas."
- The people are right: "I could not believe that instead of resisting my actions the concerned people joined me and gave me full support."

Can we manage luck?

> *"Luck is what happens when preparation meets opportunity"*

> \- Seneca

> *"I am a great believer in luck, and I find the harder I work, the more I have of it"*

> \- Thomas Jefferson

That is the big question! Can we indeed activate and control those unconceivable circumstances that determine (ultimately) a success or a failure?

A straight answer is: absolutely not, since luck is by definition the result of events beyond our understanding and control. And yet…there are maybe a few critical things that anybody can do to enhance the use or exploitation of at least 'circumstantial luck' such as:

1. Being ready when luck occurs: many people are not even aware of the fact that luck is around that they can really go for it. It is the 'right' time.
2. Spotting the opportunities that exist beyond our actions and even control: the art of taking advantage of luck is characterised by the ability that we all have (one way or another) to 'surf' on the circumstances and really 'go with the wind', building on luck.
3. Creating an environment open to luck: some actions can lead to the triggering of a set of uncontrolled events that will eventually lead to great results (the outcome of the planned actions go largely beyond what could have been expected).

On top of this, some research shows that people who believe that they are lucky are indeed luckier than those who are more pessimistic! So there is a psychological dimension to the good fortune drive: think you are lucky and it will help you!

Can bad luck be turned around?

> *"When you get to the end of your rope, tie a knot and hang on"*

> \- Franklin D. Roosevelt

The question is: How good are you at turning bad luck into an opportunity? Here are a few tested ways:

i) Fight it

Look around and you will see that some people are experiencing bad luck but they do not give up. They fight. They persevere …and it is quite amazing to see that in some cases the unlucky environment turns around and transforms itself into something positive.

ii) Go with it

Sometimes what is bad luck today can be an opportunity tomorrow. Who knows? In some cases it does pay off to be patient and just sit tight waiting for the change in fortune.

iii) Redefine it

Some bad luck forces us to have a new and fresh look at what we are facing. We may be wrong at times in the understanding of what a situation is about. The adversity can be a hidden gift.

iv) Outgrow it

Let's not get caught in the depressing feelings that bad luck can push down on us. Let's get out of the situation we are in (conceptually speaking) and project ourselves into the future. Bad luck can be a trap and one way to avoid it is to already focus on tomorrow and ignore today's dark time.

v) Neutralise it

By thinking back about our past successes and by looking at the good things that we have created through our own will and actions, we can counter-balance the negative influence of what we do not control anyway. By so doing we can minimize the effect of bad fate that is impacting us at the moment.

vi) Move around it

Taking risks in the middle of a bad luck time can push it back or around. We cannot always suffer from the negative accidental events. We must trust our good chance and move ahead on the basis of a positive probability. Let's stop procrastinating and jump over it.

vii) Rub it

We have seen people who for some un-explicable reasons are enjoying good fortunes in a systematic way. It is not a bad idea to be in their vicinity at least from time to time.

Conclusions

Luck is not something that we can ignore or neglect. It exists separately from our willpower, even if some people claim that it will be fully explained one day. We are not there yet. The notion of luck itself (and the experience of it) is still impregnated with superstition.

They say that one day what seems pure luck to us will be rationally explained and managed. They might be right. Well, in the meantime, since we are not there yet, we can only say: good luck to you!

Reader questions

1. Can you identify in your working environment a 'lucky' leader? What makes him/her lucky? How do you know that he or she is lucky?

2. Do you remember a time when - as a leader- you got lucky? What happened?

3. What is the main argument presented in the paper that you fully agree and/or disagree with?

Making leadership easy

It is commonplace when assessing leadership styles and behaviour to consider issues from the leadership perspective. We begin by considering the situation in which the leader finds himself or herself as the natural point of departure. But what about the non-leaders? For a change, let us listen to the non-leaders and learn from what they believe leadership should be. (I use the word 'non-leader' as opposed to 'follower' since in my opinion the latter is demeaning and therefore unacceptable.)

How come our leaders do not deliver the simple things that we expect from them?

Let us try, following Jack Welch's advice, to simplify leadership as much as possible and to make the art of leadership 'easy'. Yes, EASY!

Leadership has basically three dimensions:

- Strategic
- People
- Organisational

What are good (i.e. effective) leaders required to do in each dimension? Let us put ourselves in the shoes of the non-leader and see what we would expect from those who have more power than we do. Let's explore some of the key expectations that most people have of leaders.

Strategic expectations

We want our leaders to know where we are going and how we are going to get there. We want them to take charge when we are in a high risk situation and we expect them to involve us in the process of deciding on the vision and strategies when the environment is more stable and less risky.

If we push it a bit further, we would love to have a fair chance to demonstrate that we are as good as, if not better, than they.

Questions to the reader: Is that a feeling you share? Are you also experiencing that frustration?

Personal expectations

This is very simple! As team members having to report to somebody in 'authority' we have four basic necessities:

1. A fair chance to use our brainpower and talents to achieve some work objectives of which we can feel proud. Too often we feel that we do not have, especially at the beginning of our careers when we are highly motivated and energised, that legitimate opportunity to PERFORM!

2. We want to enjoy our work as well as the interface with our colleagues and other team members. We want that part of our life (i.e. our working life), to be exciting and fun. Yes ...FUN! - at least from time to time. So many leaders still behave as if others in the organisation have no feelings and emotions. What about having the chance to smile and laugh while working very hard?

3. The need to grow on the job is also something that we value. The name of the game is learning. Through on-the-job learning we improve our effectiveness, (today and tomorrow), and increase our chances of moving up the ladder and finding another interesting job elsewhere if required.

4. In many cases we think that a job should be more than a job. Honestly we are not quite motivated by the need to satisfy the shareholders' (or financial analysts') expectations. We like to think that our work is also contributing to the quality of life in our communities and societies. We love leaders who are able to show us that our contributions to the invention, production and sale of goods and services are also a way of helping people live a better life.

Challenge to the reader: Have courage and assess on a scale from 0 to 10 the ability of your leader to meet the four described expectations, where 0 indicates 'no ability' and 10 indicates 'extremely able'.

Organisational expectations

Here again our expectations are quite simple and to the point. Firstly, we want to have the proper resources and support that we need to do our job properly and effectively. We think that it is not fair to ask us to do something without giving us the relevant means, including the power, required to accomplish our objectives.

Critical point: We are getting sick and tired of the power game that our leaders are playing at our own expense.

Secondly, we expect a fair recognition and reward when the performance has been outstanding. We want fairness across the board and beyond it we want to be treated with dignity.

Critical point: We are upset by the discrepancy between the rewards the leaders apply to themselves and the rewards we get, if we get them at all. This is highly de-motivating.

Thirdly, we expect our leaders to be role-models and give the right example especially in the transformation of the corporate values into behaviours.

Critical point: It is amazing to see that so many leaders do not practice what they 'preach'. What must apply to us does not apparently apply to them.

Question for the reader: Am I going too far here? If not, and if therefore many leaders are so pathetic, why do we put up with them?

Pierre Casse

The complexity of listening: What effective leaders really do!

Three premises on listening

It seems that effective leaders keep three key ideas in mind when they communicate and these three premises have a strong impact on the way leaders relate to other people. This results in a communication process which is more authentic and creative. Effective leaders are not afraid of managing their interactions with imagination and provocation.

The three key premises are:

1. *Nature has made human beings in such a way that they cannot fully understand each other.*

    The implication for leaders is that to believe in the possibility of being able to fully and completely understand another person's mindset is nonsense. It also means that to be able to understand each other is not so vital for our survival.

2. *To invent each other while communicating is more important than to have some kind of mutual and reciprocal understanding.*

    For effective leaders, the purpose of the communication process is not to practice empathy but rather to invest time and energy in the creation of an environment from which everybody will benefit.

3. *Listening is not a process intended to encourage other people to express their ideas so that the leader can see what other people see but rather it is a process through which the leader can build on the perceptions of others and generate new and more appropriate assumptions.*

    Listening is a creative act based on a reciprocal flow of ideas that leads to the enlightenment of the parties involved and in the production of new ways to understand situations and people.

A selection of listening skills

Effective communication leaders have been using a selection of skills that range from being gently provocative to unquestionably perturbing.
Here is a sample of the listening behaviours which can provide a source of sparkling ideas:

- *Creative listening*

  The process is very simple: You say something and I pick up one word in what you said and elaborate my own ideas around that word. I'm not interested in whatever else you said and you do the same thing to me.

- *Selective listening*

  As you talk I allow my mind to wander in various directions and I react to what you say in a haphazard way. Some of your ideas trigger my own reflections and I let it happen that way.

- *Interpretative listening*

  I listen to you and in a systematic way I attribute my own meaning to what you said without trying in any way to really understand you. In other words I misunderstand you on purpose.

Are you a creative listener?

Here is a short self-assessment exercise on creative listening.
Do you agree that the following behaviours are right (acceptable) and powerful (effective)? Simply answer yes or no:

Creative listeners:	Yes	No
Give the impression that they are distracted and not listening when they actually pay full attention		
Have a tendency to guess what the speaker is going to say next		
Build their own ideas around a few words expressed by the other party and tend to neglect whatever else they say		

Creative listeners:	Yes	No
Cut people off and are impatient with slow speakers		
Misunderstand on purpose what the other person said		
Use a lot of 'yes but' statements to stimulate the other person's thinking		
Reformulate ideas/responses in the wrong way		
Use silence to encourage the speaker to say more		
Ask unexpected questions – that have nothing to do with what has been said – to challenge the other person		
Highlight and build on the contradictions in the speaker's statements		

De-briefing

- *If you have between 7 and 10 'yes' answers:* This is a bit excessive. It could be good for you to check on your own behaviours to see if they are indeed in line with your answers. If yes…think twice about the impact you could have on the people to whom you are talking.

- *If you have between 4 and 6 'yes' answers:* There is a good chance that you are both an active listener (i.e. in tune with the other person talking to you) and a creative listener (i.e. in search of new ideas). Is it really what you do in real life situations?

- *If you have between 1 and 3 'yes' answers:* This is low and it could mean that you are missing some great opportunities to trigger creativity when interacting with other people. Passive listening is not necessarily good in human communication. It is up to you to decide if it is true or not for yourself.

Beyond Blunt:
A Final Chapter

Beyond blunt:
A final chapter

"Don't confuse being stimulating with being blunt"

- Barbara Walters

This objective in this final chapter is to outline some the new, emerging ideas in the leadership field without being prescriptive in any way. In other words, this is an outline of current 'pre-trends'.

The following seven ideas may shock some people but hopefully will also stimulate thinking.

1. <u>Reverse empowerment or contingent empowerment</u>

    Reverse/contingent empowerment is evident in situations in which people tell their managers what they must do in order to prove effective. People realise that their performance is contingent upon their leader's behaviour.

2. <u>Reciprocity re-defined</u>

    More than ever before people are raising their expectations as to what the organisation must offer them as a compensation for their commitment and contribution. There is a change in perspective from "what's good for the organisation is good for you" to "what's good for me is good for the organisation".

3. <u>The death of the follower</u>

    People no longer want to be labelled as followers. The concept is obsolete. People want the opportunity from time to time to play a leadership role. So the responsibility of the team leader is no longer to develop followers but to create leaders.

4. <u>Leadership velocity</u>

    Leaders are experiencing what we can call fast rotation. Today the power in most teams and organisations moves around form one person to another according to the requirements of the situations with which the team/organisation is faced at a given moment.

5.   The curse of irreversibility

Leaders must act according to decisions that have been made some time ago. Their choices are limited and they must learn how to minimise the negative consequences of decisions that were perhaps appropriate at the time but no longer meet the requirements of a new environment. Moreover, leaders often face the challenge of having to turn transform the inappropriate into the appropriate.

6.   Mistakes into opportunities

The time when a leader could say "I can make mistakes as long as I learn from them and I do not repeat them" is over. In a fast changing world this is attitude is unacceptable. The only acceptable mistake a leader can make is the one that he or she turns into an opportunity. It may not be easy but this doesn't mean it's not feasible. It only requires imagination and a bit of courage.

7.   From 'box' to 'no box'

The ubiquitous refrain, "think outside the box" is redundant. The real leaders are those who are creating the new boxes and fuelling the re-invention of the business world by so doing. Moreover, it seems that the future belongs to those emerging leaders who can live and contribute without the need for boxes.

The 'final' leadership test!

Here is an opportunity for you, the reader, to test your own ability to challenge the traditional way of looking at leadership. Consider the extent to which you feel comfortable with the statements listed hereunder using the following scale as a guide. Choose any number between 1 and 10.

1 = not at all uncomfortable
5 = a bit uncomfortable
10 = very much uncomfortable

	Score
Leadership is about serving others	
Leadership is ultimately about power	
Leaders are not born; they invent themselves	
Organisations exist to serve people, not the reverse	
A high IQ is not good from a leadership perspective	
Effective leaders are good at paying special attention to people's emotions	
Good leaders are re-inventing themselves all the time	
A leader without flair or intuition is a poor leader	
Successful leadership is based on helping others to be great	
Sound leaders know that power corrupts	
To be provocative can be a very effective leadership tool	
Great leaders cannot stand the tyranny of the average	
Forget about people's weaknesses; leaders focus on strengths	
The separation between private and professional life is schizophrenic	
Human communication is such that we cannot understand each other	
Teamwork has been overvalued by shy leaders	
To be provocative is a leadership key success factor	
To create a mind expansion environment at work is the key challenge for leaders	
Not to know is good from a leadership perspective	
Women are better leaders than men	
Total score	

De-briefing

- *For a score between 150 and 200:* You are hopeless. Forget about leadership.

- *For a score between 50 and 150:* Do you really know who you are as a leader? I doubt it. Go back to some of the key items and check again.

- *For a score between 20 and 50:* This is too wild. Either you are lying or you are sick!

The "ultimate" leadership hurdle

Consider the following leadership dilemmas and for each situation, try to identify what you would do if you were the leader in question.

Dilemma 1

As a corporate leader, you go to a meeting to present some revolutionary ideas about the business and you know that most of the managers in the room will be negative and block your ideas. What should you do?

Do you:

1.   Make sure that the meeting is postponed?
2.   Go to the meeting with a fighting spirit?
3.   Present the ideas in a low key way?

Or if you would handle the situation in another way, what would you do?

Dilemma 2

One of your team members has made a serious mistake that will almost certainly jeopardise the success of a very important project. You recruited him and he is a close friend of yours. What do you think you should do next?

Do you:

1.   Take over the project and try to save it?
2.   Just wait and see what will happen next?
3.   Have a straight conversation with the team member?

Or if you would handle the situation in another way, what would you do?

Dilemma 3

Research shows that only 40 % of the talents that exist in successful organisations are recognised and used.

Do you:

1. Believe it?
2. Question it? Should it be less than 40%?
3. Ignore such research because you are not interested in it?

Or if you would handle the situation in another way, what would you do?

Dilemma 4

The situation you are facing in your organisation is full of ambiguity. You must make a decision quickly. It could go very well but it could also destroy your organisation. It seems that you have no choice.

Do you:

1. Challenge the urgency of the situation?
2. Trust your intuition and decide on the spot?
3. Ask for advice?

Or if you would handle the situation in another way, what would you do?

Dilemma 5

Your direct boss blames you for a bad decision that he has made. The situation is very serious. The consequences for the organization will be dramatic and it seems that somebody must take responsibility.

Do you:

1. Get ready to 'pay' for your boss's mistake?
2. Make sure that everybody knows that it is not your mistake?
3. Try to 'pass the buck' to somebody else?

Or if you would handle the situation in another way, what would you do?

Dilemma 6

You are sick and tired of working in your organisation. You do not enjoy your job anymore.

Do you:

1. Try to redesign your job?
2. Look for another assignment within the organisation?
3. Just quit?

Or if you would handle the situation in another way, what would you do?

Dilemma 7

Your spouse is very upset about the fact that you are working overtime and that you do not pay much attention to your family anymore. He/she is really concerned about your relationship.

Do you:

1. Tell your spouse that everything will be fine?
2. Promise to change things around?
3. Talk to your boss about it?

Or if you would handle the situation in another way, what would you do?

De-briefing

Examine your answers and assess each one on the following scale:
1 = very conventional
5 = a mix of conventional and unconventional
10 = very unconventional

Is there a pattern emerging? What is this exercise telling you about your leadership mind-set?

Challenge yourself by creating your own seven dilemmas! Keep in mind that 'mentalising' is the key to survival and success.